And
Still I Cook

And
Still I Cook

Leah Chase

Forewords by
Don Rousell and Jan Waddy

PELICAN PUBLISHING COMPANY
Gretna 2011

First printing, May 2003
Second printing, January 2006
First paperback edition, July 2011

Library of Congress Cataloging-in-Publication Data

Chase, Leah.
  And still I cook / Leah Chase ; forewords by Don Rousell and Jan
Waddy.
      p. cm.
Includes index.
  ISBN-13: 9781455615605
  1. Cookery, American—Louisiana style. 2. Cookery, Creole. 3. Dooky
Chase (Restaurant) I. Title.
  TX715.2.L68 C39 2003
  641.59763—dc21

                                        2002152277

Printed in the United States of America

Published by Pelican Publishing Company, Inc.
1000 Burmaster Street, Gretna, Louisiana 70053

CONTENTS

FOREWORD

When I think of Leah Chase, almost immediately I am smiling. You see, I have had the wonderful pleasure of being both Leah's co-host and co-executive producer of her television series, "Creole Cooking with Leah Chase." This placed me in the unique position of being both business partner and surrogate son. Our love and respect for each other is rooted in our mutual love, respect, and consumption of food—wonderful Creole food. Simply put, Leah cooks, and I eat.

From the beginning of our relationship, Leah was the teacher and I was the student. And this was a class from which I never wanted to play hooky. Over the years, Leah has advised me to run the gamut, from cooking to politics, relationships to business, and, most importantly, family to friends. However, most of our conversations centered around food and the importance of getting friends back to the table. Usually, I was eating while Leah would nurse an iced tea. My standing order is Leah's Creole gumbo, chock-full of fresh large Gulf shrimp, sausage, crabs, and Leah's dangerous garlic bread—on the side, that is. To this day I love it! If you ever visit her family's restaurant, Dooky Chase in New Orleans, and you've been good, treat yourself. Then tell your friends; they will love you for it.

You know, one must pause at the spectacle of it all. Leah is one of the most humble persons I have ever known. To this day she is surprised at her celebrity. I remember clearly the first time Leah and I spoke about doing a cooking series. We were sitting in the gold room at Dooky Chase, where she has been executive chef since the 1950s. I asked, "Leah, have you ever thought about doing a cooking series of your own? After all, you have been on air with everyone from Julia Child to Graham Kerr. I think people would watch it, and everybody loves you." Leah's response almost knocked me out. "Do you think anyone would give us the money to do it?" *"What?!"* I thought to myself.

The rest, as they say, is history. Leah did get her series. It was broadcast nationally on PBS, Discovery Channel Digital, and the Home & Leisure Channel. And I'll say it was long overdue, not just because Leah is such a gifted artist but because she is a true American in every sense of the word: a pioneer, wife, mother, grandmother, and friend to many. She was a voice in the community when African-American voices weren't welcome. There are many things Leah has to share, and they start at the dinner table. Her goal is to bring families together again and that's a good thing. So, look through this book. Find a recipe your family or friends will like, pull up a couple of chairs, and let the conversations begin. If you listen closely, you just might hear Leah.

Don Rousell

Being a member of a large family is a mixed blessing, and at times I wonder if being the youngest of eleven girls is something just shy of a curse. Nonetheless, that's where I am, and I feel privileged to be a part of this clan of fun-loving, awe-inspiring men and women.

For Daddy and Mother, my birth must have been somebody's idea of a cruel joke. They surely must have thought their luck had changed when, after ten girls, the first son was born. Well, I certainly fixed that when I plopped right in after Charles. Three years later, Hayes was born.

I come right between the two sons, and I readily admit I'm a tomboy. The "boys" are spoiled, and since I'm the youngest female, I believe that my sisters still think of me as their "little" sister. The tomboy in me allows for some interesting memories and a strong relationship with my brothers; being the youngest girl gives me a unique perspective on womanhood. I've had a total of nine (including Mother) very strong women to influence me. (The other two sisters died before I was born.)

It's not a bad spot to be in, actually, because I confide in and rely on every one of my siblings whenever I need to. That is the blessing of a family like ours.

There is an eighteen-year difference between my sister Leah and me. That makes for some interesting conversations, especially when it comes to how we were raised. Of course, older sisters claim that the younger ones got away with bloody murder, but I can attest to the fact that we were definitely not exempt from the strict discipline of our parents, and in addition to punishment from Mother and Daddy, we were also subject to being disciplined by our older siblings.

With that discipline, though, came a sense of respect that is irreplaceable. I am old enough to remember the struggles Leah went through to make Dooky Chase's the first-class restaurant it has become. I am smart enough to recognize and take advantage of all the learning opportunities afforded by her experiences.

It is an honor to collaborate on this second book and an immense pleasure to have the time to share more deeply in what is her passion.

Jan Waddy

PREFACE

In my first cookbook, *The Dooky Chase Cookbook,* the origin of Dooky Chase's was highlighted in the preface. More than fifty years have gone by since I first put spoon to pot in the restaurant business. I've learned a lot of lessons, mostly the hard way. The restaurant business is a hard life. In spite of the difficulties and disappointments, I'd do it all again, but maybe a little differently.

Since the 1950s, I've seen a lot of changes take place in the world. I've seen people—especially black people—come into their own, into their rightful places in society. I've seen changes in the way people do business. I've implemented more than a few changes in the way we do business at Dooky's. It's a necessity if your goal is to stay in business.

As inevitable as change is, there are some things that should never change. I've tried to hold on to those things because they've been my mainstay—things like honesty and giving credit where it's due; things like faith and common courtesy; like knowing the importance of balancing family and business.

I've learned some valuable lessons about running a family-owned business. The most important lesson is that you must separate the two. You must forget that this is family when it comes to doing business, and you must remember to play an integral part in family at home. You cannot put all the focus just on the business.

The pages in this book are filled with the influence of fifty years of family and business. The recipes are part family, part experimentation, part honest hard work. I hope that when you try these recipes, they will become one of the ingredients that brings your family together to celebrate one another.

ACKNOWLEDGMENTS

Remember you're never too old to learn; you're never too young to teach.
—Jan Waddy

It's amazing to me that every day of your life, there's something new to learn. It doesn't matter how old or young you are. Learning is the passport to making you a better person. I learned that a long time ago from Mother. I try hard to make that a legacy for my children and my children's children.

Something else I've learned is that you cannot afford to wait another day to tell those you love how much they mean to you. There are no guarantees given to the length of a life. Each new day is an opportunity to give a little more. I didn't fully realize that until death came way too soon and snatched our daughter Emily from us.

Most people think of death as the final separation of the living, but death impacts the way you live your life. It directs your thinking and your actions. You see life differently after someone close to you has died.

Our daughter Emily spent a lot of time in this restaurant. She was such a special blessing for me. She knew exactly where I was coming from and would use that diplomacy she was so famous for to make me look at a problem from a different perspective.

When Em died, I thought my world would fall apart. I did the only thing I could do. I cooked. I lost myself in the pots. Some people might think that it was an unhealthy thing to do, but I believe it was what saved me from total destruction.

We take so much for granted in life. Not in a million years would I have dreamed that Emily would precede me in death. It is just not supposed to happen that parents bury their children. But the more I thought about it, the more I came to realize I'm not in charge of life and death. Only God has that power, and no matter how long or hard I think and pray, that will never change.

I choose to spend my time these days thinking of the lessons that Em taught. Your children teach such profound lessons. She still inspires me daily and the most valued lesson is this: We take for granted that our loved ones will be with us day in and day out, so much so that we do not spend the time to share ourselves with them.

Em's death forces me to think about her every day, and I know that will always be the case. Most important of all, her death has made me more keenly aware of all the miraculous things that surround me—from the beauty of flowers that some would call weeds to the wonderful people who are part of my life. What a blessing it is to really understand that. It is the best tribute I can pay to Emily. She knew it all along.

There are so many people who have helped make my journey a joyful one. A countless number of people have helped me in the kitchen, in the business, and in life. I am grateful to them all.

I really don't like to single people out, but sometimes you just have to acknowledge those people who play a significant role in shaping your success.

My family is a true blessing. To have the privilege of loving support and encouragement, not just in this endeavor but in life, is a wonderful gift. Thank you for being there for me.

I especially thank Dr. Milburn Calhoun for his patience, his helpfulness, and his Southern gentility. Thanks too to those people in the arts who put a touch of soft and simple elegance in my life, providing a place for me to find respite and renewal.

To Bishop Anderson, Father Michael, Stella and Ella, Clifton, John, a wonderful lady we simply call Sunny, and all the many others whose names could fill more pages than this book can contain, thank you for caring and for helping me to understand the language of unconditional love.

I am also grateful to all those who will buy and use this book. I hope you realize the abundant blessings possible when you pour yourself into whatever it is you do, and I do hope you will put at least a little bit of yourselves into your cooking.

Finally, to all those seemingly insignificant people whose lives have intersected mine, no matter how briefly or how small, thank you for giving me priceless insight and great meaning in life.

It is such an honor for me to share this time and space with all of you. Thank you.

INTRODUCTION

My parents firmly believed in the importance of teaching their children those timeless values that would help them become productive adults. Their lessons were driven home by any means possible. Sometimes it was with words, sometimes with their hands or the closest thing they could reach with their hands.

Mother concentrated on manners. We had little more than an oilcloth table covering during the depression, and the wash bench doubled as seating for our meals, but Mother insisted that we sit up straight at the table, hold our eating utensils correctly, and keep our elbows off the table. Even though she had not completed elementary school, she knew the value of good manners and courtesy. She would correct our speech as much as her sixth-grade education would allow.

Not even Daddy was exempt from her admonishment if he mispronounced words. Of course, Daddy would know exactly how to turn Mother's scolding into lightheartedness. He would often mispronounce a word just to hear her fuss. For example, he would say to one of us, "Come heah," in the broken English that was common in those days. Mother, not having any of that, would say, "Charles, it's 'here' not 'heah.'" Daddy would grin and say, "Okay . . . come hither."

As much as Mother was concerned about politeness and manners, Daddy was concerned about the importance of knowing how to "figure." He taught us all how to count and say our alphabets before we started school. If he sent one of us to the store, he made sure we counted out the exact change coming to us. "That way," he cautioned, "you'll never let anyone cheat you."

My parents taught mostly by example. Daddy believed in giving people more than they expected. When he harvested vegetables from the garden, people would come to buy from him because they knew he would sell only the most tender green beans and okra or the firmest tomatoes. He'd always give something extra—a seasoning bunch or a handful of freshly picked cayenne peppers. In this area it's called giving a little lagniappe. We could plainly see from his example that his motto was *Give the best of whatever it is you have to give.*

Both Mother and Daddy taught us about work ethic. If something wasn't done to their satisfaction, then it had to be done over until it was right. Mother worked meticulously whether she was sewing or preparing food, and Daddy's garden was picture perfect in even rows and without a trace of weeds. Tools were always cleaned and sharpened before they were put away.

They also gave education a high priority. After the dinner table was cleared, we would all get out our books to "do our lessons." The older ones were expected to help the younger ones. If one of us got into trouble at school, there would be the devil to pay when we got home.

Once, Mr. Talley, the principal at the white school just across the field from our house, was throwing some books on the trash pile to be burned. Daddy had no idea what those books were, but he took the wheelbarrow and went to retrieve them. As it turned out, there were readers and a two-volume set of dictionaries in the pile. We spent the summer going through each one of those books. The dictionary set was placed in the rolltop desk as a reference.

Daddy finished only the third grade, but he never stopped learning. He always had his Bible study book handy for reading after his day's work. He also read the newspaper every day. If he ran across a word he didn't understand, he would call one of the children and ask the meaning of that word. He was never too proud to ask for help when he needed it.

This is how we grew up: learning to give of ourselves, sharing what we had, and understanding that learning is important. It is undeniably a part of who I am today.

Using these tools in the restaurant business has brought me through some rough spots. Looking back, I realize they have served me well.

And
Still I Cook

ABBREVIATIONS

Standard

tsp.	=	teaspoon
tbsp.	=	tablespoon
oz.	=	ounce
qt.	=	quart
lb.	=	pound

Metric

ml.	=	milliliter
l.	=	liter
g.	=	gram
kg.	=	kilogram
mg.	=	milligram

STANDARD-METRIC APPROXIMATIONS

$\frac{1}{8}$ teaspoon	=	.6 milliliter		
$\frac{1}{4}$ teaspoon	=	1.2 milliliters		
$\frac{1}{2}$ teaspoon	=	2.5 milliliters		
1 teaspoon	=	5 milliliters		
1 tablespoon	=	15 milliliters		
4 tablespoons	=	$\frac{1}{4}$ cup	=	60 milliliters
8 tablespoons	=	$\frac{1}{2}$ cup	=	118 milliliters
16 tablespoons	=	1 cup	=	236 milliliters
2 cups	=	473 milliliters		
$2\frac{1}{2}$ cups	=	563 milliliters		
4 cups	=	946 milliliters		
1 quart	=	4 cups	=	.94 liter

SOLID MEASUREMENTS

$\frac{1}{2}$ ounce	=	15 grams		
1 ounce	=	25 grams		
4 ounces	=	110 grams		
16 ounces	=	1 pound	=	454 grams

Breakfast

How far you go in life depends on your being tender with the young, compassionate with the aged, sympathetic with the striving, and tolerant with the weak and strong. Because someday in your life, you will have been all of these.   —George Washington Carver

I love that quote by George Washington Carver. Sometimes in one day I am all of those things.

In spite of all the obstacles he faced, Carver still had the courage to keep doing what he believed in. He was a man driven by the need to make life better for the members of his community. We owe a debt of gratitude to all those who have gone before us with that same philosophy. The best way we can repay that debt is to strive to do the same.

The walls of Dooky Chase are adorned with plaques and awards we've received over the years. My favorite is the Loving Cup because it speaks to the idea of building community. I think everybody should have a plaque hanging on their wall. Everybody has the chance to be involved in something that is worthy and honorable. Everybody can do something that will make things better for those who follow, not so much because it brings individual honor, but because it brings you the opportunity to share the glory with all the members of your community. So when you receive your honors, receive them in the name of everyone who has helped you.

Dooky's has been located in the same place in New Orleans for all these years. We've never had a restaurant in our particular community that's lasted this long. It would have been easy to relocate to what some would call a "better" place. I am a part of this community. I love the people here, and if there is any legacy I leave, it will be that I tried to uplift the people of my community. It's up to us to make everyone living in a community realize how important it is to them.

We are surrounded by the projects and small houses. Some people don't understand that you have to take a chance on humanity. They come to Dooky's and they see the restaurant in a low-income neighborhood. They say to themselves, "What's going on here?"

It's an opportunity for them to learn. I come from poor beginnings. I know what it's like to be the underdog. I understand that just because you're poor does not mean you have to be without respect or dignity, does not mean that you cannot do good for others, does not mean that you are not honest and courageous. If there is anything I can do to help others understand that same philosophy, then I must do it.

That's what these awards mean to me. I am a part of this community. I want people to see that these plaques and awards are for all of us who live in this community. The folks here supported Dooky's when it was a struggling sandwich shop, and they still support us today. This restaurant stands as a testament to that support. These awards tell the story of that support and lift us all up a little higher. I am honored and humbled to be a part of this community's growth and achievement.

CREOLE OMELET

This omelet is turned over on the platter after being filled. But as I remember, Mother never folded omelets over. They were just cooked and served with the mixture on top!

½ stick butter
1 cup chopped ripe fresh tomatoes
¼ cup chopped onions
½ cup chopped ham
2 cloves garlic, mashed and
   chopped

½ tsp. black pepper
1 tsp. salt
⅓ cup chopped bell pepper
6 eggs, beaten

Put 1 tbsp. of butter in pan, heat over a medium fire, and add tomatoes, onions, ham, garlic, ½ tsp. salt, and ¼ tsp. black pepper. Cook for 10 minutes and add bell peppers. Cook about 3 minutes until bell peppers are barely soft and set aside.

In a large skillet, heat remaining butter over a medium fire. Season eggs with remaining salt and pepper. Pour eggs into hot skillet. Stir eggs to cover skillet bottom so they can cook evenly. Then pour tomato mixture over eggs. Let eggs cook until hard, about 4-5 minutes, and turn over on platter.

Serves 4.

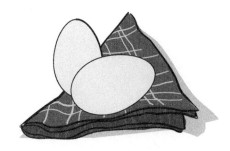

OYSTER OMELET

1 tbsp. butter
1 doz. plump oysters with liquid
1 tbsp. chopped green onions
½ tsp. salt

1 tsp. white pepper
1 tsp. butter
6 eggs, well beaten
Chopped parsley for garnish

Melt 1 tbsp. butter in a skillet over a high fire. Drain oysters and save the liquid. Chop oysters and set aside. To melted butter add green onion and oyster liquid; stir constantly. Add oysters and cook for 5 minutes. Add salt and pepper and set aside.

Heat 1 tsp. butter in a skillet over a medium fire and add the eggs, rolling eggs up the side of the pan. When eggs set, spoon half the oyster mixture in the middle and fold omelet over oysters. Remove omelet from skillet and spoon remaining oyster mixture over the omelet. Garnish with chopped parsley.

Serves 4.

STRAWBERRY OMELET

½ stick butter
½ pt. ripe strawberries, sliced
1 tbsp. sugar
1 tbsp. Cointreau (liquor)

4 eggs, beaten
½ tsp. salt
1 level tbsp. self-rising flour

Heat half the butter in a small skillet over a medium-high fire. Add strawberries, sugar, and Cointreau. Cook for 5 minutes and set aside.

To beaten eggs, add salt and flour. Continue to beat until mixture is smooth. Heat remaining butter in a skillet over a medium fire. Pour egg mixture in the hot skillet, rolling eggs up the sides and pulling them down with a fork. Cook about 4-5 minutes until eggs set. Pour half the strawberry mixture in the middle of the omelet, fold omelet over strawberry mixture, and turn over on a plate. Pour remaining strawberries over the omelet.

Serves 4.

JAM OMELET

4 eggs
2 tbsp. milk
3 tbsp. strawberry or your
   favorite jam

1 tbsp. butter

Beat eggs well. Stir in milk and jam and mix well. Heat butter in a skillet over a medium fire, pour in eggs, and stir well. Let set and cook about 4-5 minutes. Turn omelet over onto a hot plate. May be served with biscuits or toast.

Serves 4.

EGGS IN TOMATOES

¼ cup finely chopped onions
3 cups whole tomatoes
1 tsp. Lawry's Seasoned Salt
¼ tsp. cayenne pepper
½ tsp. chopped garlic

1 tbsp. chopped parsley
½ cup water
4 eggs
French bread slices

Spray a large skillet with nonstick cooking spray and heat over a medium fire. Add onions and cook about 5 minutes until they are clear. Add tomatoes, breaking them up with a spoon as you stir and cook. Add salt, cayenne, garlic, parsley, and water and bring mixture to a boil. Break the eggs one at a time in the boiling tomato sauce, taking care not to break the yolks. Turn to a low fire and cook slowly until whites are set. Serve over slices of French bread.

Serves 4.

RED ONION AND POTATO SCRAMBLE

¼ cup vegetable oil
6 eggs, beaten
1 large red onion, chopped
2 cups diced cooked frozen
   French fries

1 tsp. salt
1 tsp. black pepper

Heat oil in a large skillet over a high fire. To beaten eggs add onions and potatoes and beat in salt and pepper. Pour into the hot skillet and move the mixture around so it can scramble and set, about 3 minutes. Serve on a warm platter.

Serves 4.

BAKED CHEESE GRITS WITH JALAPENO PEPPERS

2 cups yellow grits
4 cups cold water
1 cup shredded cheddar cheese
1 tsp. Lawry's Seasoned Salt
½ cup heavy cream

2 eggs, beaten
¼ cup chopped jalapeño peppers
Butter for greasing
Paprika and parsley for garnish

Cook grits over a high fire in water, stirring well, until it boils. Lower fire and cook for 15 minutes. Remove from fire and add cheese and seasoned salt.

Add cream to eggs and stir well. Add peppers. Pour into grits and stir well.

Grease a Pyrex baking dish with butter and pour in grits. Sprinkle with paprika and parsley. Bake at 375 degrees for 20 minutes.

Serves 4.

HERBED GRITS

2 cups grits
6 cups cold water
1 tsp. whole thyme leaves

¼ tsp. Herbes de Provence
1 tsp. salt
1 tbsp. butter

Pour grits in a pot and add water. Stir in herbs and salt and bring to a boil. Stir well and lower fire. Cook for 15 minutes. Add butter and cook for another 5 minutes.

Serves 4.

FRIED GRITS CAKES WITH ROSEMARY AND BLUE CHEESE

2 cups grits
4 cups cold water
1 tsp. salt
¼ tsp. cayenne pepper
1 tbsp. chopped rosemary
½ cup crumbled blue cheese

1 egg, beaten
1 cup evaporated milk
½ cup water
2 cups white cornmeal
Deep fat for frying

Stir grits into the 4 cups water and add salt. Bring to a boil. Stir well to keep grits smooth. Lower fire; cook slowly for 15 minutes.

Stir in cayenne, rosemary, and blue cheese and whip grits well. Pour grits into a well-greased square pan, to about ½ inch thick. Refrigerate overnight.

Cut grits in squares, then halve squares diagonally, to form two triangles each. In a bowl, add egg to milk. Mix in the ½ cup water and stir well. Dip grits in milk mixture, then into cornmeal, coating well. Fry in deep fat at 350 to 375 degrees until coating is crisp, about 3 minutes per side.

Serves 4.

RICE PANCAKES WITH HAM AND TOMATO-BASIL SAUCE

2 cups cooked rice
½ cup self-rising flour
1 tbsp. salt
½ tsp. white pepper

2 eggs, beaten
½ cup milk
¼ cup shortening

Pour rice in a bowl and add flour, salt, and pepper. Mix well.

Slowly add eggs. Continue to stir. Add milk and whip well.

Heat shortening over a high fire in a heavy skillet or on a griddle. Spoon pancakes onto greased surface. Brown on one side, about 4 minutes, then turn and brown about 4 minutes on the other side. Place pancakes on a warm platter.

HAM AND TOMATO-BASIL SAUCE

Heat butter over a medium-low fire in a skillet. Add ham and toss

1 tbsp. butter
½ lb. cooked ham, chopped
2 cups chopped ripe fresh tomatoes with seeds
4 green onions, chopped

2 fresh jalapeño peppers, seeded and chopped
1 tsp. chopped basil
½ tsp. garlic salt

around, but do not brown. Raise fire to medium. Add tomatoes, green onions, and peppers and sauté about 5 minutes. Lower fire. Add basil and garlic salt and cook 5 minutes. Serve over rice pancakes.

Serves 4.

PLAIN OLD FRITTERS

This was our breakfast on many cold mornings. Mother served these with cane syrup.

2 cups self-rising flour
2 tbsp. sugar
1 egg, beaten

1¼ cups milk
1 tsp. vanilla
Hot oil for frying

Sift flour in a bowl. Add sugar, egg, milk, and vanilla. Mix until you have a smooth batter. Heat oil over a high fire to 375 degrees. Drop spoonfuls in hot oil, turning with a spatula to brown on each side, about 3 minutes per side. Drain on paper towel.

Serves 4.

Sandwiches

A pork chop po' boy
. . . sheer joy.

Sandwiches go all the way back to the 1700s. When the Earl of
Sandwich was too involved in playing cards to eat a meal, he asked
a servant to bring him a piece of meat with bread. That, history tells us, is
the origin of the sandwich.

Every self-respecting New Orleanian knows that you haven't eaten a real
sandwich until you've had a New Orleans-style po' boy. There's nothing
like eating hot and juicy meat or seafood on a crisp loaf of po'-boy bread.
We've cornered a bit of history ourselves when it comes to sandwich making. It was more out of necessity than pleasure.

When blacks took in washing for others, they invented the means to feed
their children and save time in the process. Often, they would put a pot of
beans on the stove early in the morning because the beans didn't need a lot
of tending. Then they would start scrubbing clothes on those old wooden
washboards.

Around noon, when the children got hungry, the mother would take a
loaf of French bread, scoop out the middle, and fill the hollowed bread with
beans. She would give each child a piece and get back to washing clothes.

The idea of eating cold cuts on a piece of bread is almost blasphemous to
most good cooks around here. We like our sandwiches with lots of sub-
stance. Fried oyster and shrimp po' boys are the most popular, but we make
all kinds of hot, "stick to the ribs" sandwiches.

One day, years ago, a man from across the street came into Dooky Chase's
and asked for a Hungry Man Sandwich. I didn't have a clue as to what that
was, let alone how to fix it. So I did the only sensible thing I could do. I
asked him. He let me know that a Hungry Man was French fries on French
bread, fully dressed. (In New Orleans, a "dressed" sandwich includes mayonnaise, lettuce, tomatoes, and pickles.) When he gave me that piece of
information, I learned more than what a Hungry Man Sandwich was. I

learned that I belonged to this unique community. The people were willing to share their knowledge with me. The next time someone came in and asked for a Hungry Man Sandwich, and I could fix it with confidence, I felt like a queen. It's the little things, the simple things, more often than not, that make a place or person unique.

These recipes for sandwiches are sure to please any appetite.

FRIED SHRIMP SANDWICH

½ lb. shrimp, peeled and
   deveined
Salt and pepper to taste
2 cups vegetable oil
¼ cup evaporated milk
1 tsp. catsup

¼ tsp. Tabasco sauce
1 cup yellow cornmeal
French bun or any crusty bread,
   split lengthwise
1 tbsp. butter
Mayonnaise

Wash shrimp and season with salt and pepper.

Heat oil to 375 degrees over a high fire in a skillet.

Mix milk, catsup, and Tabasco. Pour over shrimp and mix well. Take shrimp from milk and shake in cornmeal, coating shrimp well. Fry shrimp until done, about 5 minutes.

Toast bread halves. Spread butter on bottom half and place shrimp on it. Spread mayonnaise on the other half. Place this half on the shrimp to make a delicious sandwich.

Serves 1.

MINCED OYSTERS ON TOAST

1 doz. oysters with liquid
2 tbsp. butter
3 green onions with bottoms,
   chopped

Salt and pepper to taste
1 tsp. chopped parsley
6 slices dry toast

Put oysters and liquid in small pot and let come to a boil. Cook a few minutes until oysters just curl on the edges. Drain oysters, saving liquid.

Heat butter over a medium fire in a skillet and add green onions. Lower fire and cook slowly, about 5 minutes.

Mince oysters. Add to onions with reserved liquid and cook for 5 minutes on a high fire, stirring constantly. Add salt, pepper, and parsley. Spoon mixture on 3 toast slices. Cover with the other toast slices to complete the sandwiches.

Serves 3.

PORK CHOP AND OYSTER PO' BOY

This is my all-time favorite sandwich!

2 boneless pork chops	½ cup yellow cornmeal
Salt and pepper to taste	2 6-in. pieces French bread or 2
1 cup vegetable oil	French rolls, split lengthwise
6 plump oysters	Cold butter

With the heel of your hand, pound chops to make them just a little thinner. Season with salt and pepper.

Heat oil to 375 degrees over a high fire in a small frying pan and fry chops until light brown on both sides, about 5 minutes per side. Remove chops and keep warm on the side.

Drain oysters and dredge in cornmeal, covering well. Fry oysters over a high fire in same oil that the chops were cooked in. Cook until crispy on outsides, about 6 minutes.

Heat bread. Spread cold butter on all slices. Place pork chops on bottom halves. Lay oysters on top of chops. Cover with buttered top halves of bread.

Serves 2.

HAM SANDWICH

When I was growing up in Madisonville, Louisiana, there was little for men to do for entertainment. But when Saturday night came, Daddy would go to the only bar in town. Men always brought a treat home for their wives.

All I ever remember Mother asking for was a ham sandwich. She always thought that was special. It took so little to make Mother happy. I can see her now, patiently waiting until twelve at night for that ham sandwich.

French bun, toasted	1 thin slice ham
Mayonnaise	Creole mustard

Spread bottom half of bun lightly with mayonnaise. Stack on ham. Spread mustard on top half of bun and cover bottom. Voila! Mother's treat.

Serves 1.

BISCUIT SANDWICHES

Many mornings, a biscuit sandwich and a cup of cocoa was my breakfast before school. This meager breakfast was no excuse for low grades. You were expected to do above average.

1 tbsp. mayonnaise	**4 leftover biscuits**
1 tsp. butter, softened	**4 thin slices ripe tomato**
4 strips bacon	

Mix butter and mayonnaise and set aside.

Cook bacon until crisp.

Cut biscuits open and toast until nice and brown. Spread mayonnaise mixture on each half. Break slices of bacon onto 4 biscuit bottoms. Place tomatoes over bacon. Cover with biscuit tops and serve very hot.

Serves 4.

VARIATION

4 leftover biscuits	**Strawberry preserves**
Butter, softened	

Cut cold biscuits open and butter both sides. Spread preserves on 4 biscuit bottoms and cover with biscuit tops to make sandwiches.

Serves 4.

SARDINES AND RED ONIONS ON FRENCH BREAD

6-in. piece French bread	**3 thin slices red onion**
1 can sardines packed in oil	**Generous dash Tabasco sauce**

Split bread lengthwise. Lay sardines on bottom half, pouring the oil over the sardines. Place onions over sardines. Add Tabasco. Cover with top half of bread.

Serves 1.

HUNGRY MAN SANDWICH

8-in. piece French bread, split
  lengthwise
Mayonnaise
Cooked French fries

Salt and pepper to taste
Shredded lettuce
Sliced tomatoes
Sliced pickles

Heat bread and spread both halves with mayonnaise. Place French fries on bottom half. Season with salt and pepper and top with lettuce, tomatoes, and pickles. Cover to make the sandwich complete!

Serves 1.

VARIATION

Pizza sauce
Tabasco sauce
8-in. piece French bread, split
  lengthwise

Cooked French fries
Shredded mozzarella cheese
Shredded cheddar cheese
Chopped parsley

Mix pizza sauce with Tabasco. Be generous with the Tabasco.

Spread each bread half with pizza sauce. Place fries on both halves. Mix cheeses together and cover fries with cheese mixture. Sprinkle with chopped parsley.

Bake halves in the oven at 350 degrees for about 15 minutes. Once cheese is melted, cut halves into 2-in. pieces and serve.

Serves 1.

BREADED CHICKEN LIVERS ON TOAST

½ cup evaporated milk
1 egg, beaten
¼ cup water
6 chicken livers
Lawry's Seasoned Salt

Breadcrumbs
1 cup oil or bacon fat
Mayonnaise
Toasted white bread slices

Mix milk and egg in a bowl. Add water. Dip chicken livers in the milk. Remove livers and season them with seasoned salt. Shake livers in breadcrumbs. Heat oil over a high fire and fry livers until done (about 10 minutes). Drain livers. Spread a little mayonnaise on toast. Place livers between slices of toast. Now you're ready to eat!

PARTY SHRIMP SANDWICH

Every month, the volunteer committee at the New Orleans Museum of Art has a meeting. My job at these meetings is to make the lunches.

For general meetings, which are held three times a year, I make about one thousand party sandwiches. I really enjoy this. I get to make a lot of creative fillings!

1½ sticks butter, softened
¼ tsp. mace
¼ tsp. cayenne pepper
½ tsp. Lawry's Seasoned Salt

3 cups small shrimp, boiled,
    peeled, and deveined
6 slices rye bread

Mix butter with mace, cayenne, and seasoned salt.

Chop shrimp a little and add to butter mixture. Spread shrimp mixture on bread, making nice full sandwiches. Cut in small squares.

Serves 3.

SPINACH SANDWICHES

2 lb. fresh spinach	1 tbsp. vegetable oil
8 oz. cream cheese, softened	1 tsp. vinegar
½ tsp. white pepper	8 white bread slices

Remove large stems from spinach and discard stems. Wash leaves and drain well. Pat dry with a cloth. Chop spinach into small pieces.

In a large bowl, mix cream cheese, pepper, oil, and vinegar. Mix well and toss chopped spinach in. Mix until a smooth spread.

Trim crusts from bread. Spread spinach mixture on bread and cover to make sandwiches. Cut each sandwich into 4 nice triangles.

Serves 4.

BROCCOLI SANDWICHES

2 bunches broccoli	1 tbsp. ranch salad dressing
½ cup Italian salad dressing	6 slices whole-wheat bread slices,
1 stick butter, softened	trimmed
2 tbsp. mayonnaise	Ranch dressing for dip

Cut flowerets from broccoli stems. Peel stems and cut them in thin sticks. Wash well and drain. Place broccoli flowerets and sticks in bowl. Pour Italian dressing over broccoli and stir so all broccoli is coated. Cover with plastic wrap and place in the refrigerator overnight.

In a small bowl, mix butter, mayonnaise, and 1 tbsp. ranch dressing until smooth.

Drain broccoli well. Spread bread with butter mixture. Place broccoli on 3 slices and cover with other slices to make sandwiches. Cut each sandwich in fours. Arrange on a plate and garnish with broccoli stick and a small cup of ranch dressing for dipping.

Serves 3.

BLUE CHEESE SANDWICHES

6 slices pumpernickel bread
Butter, softened
1 cup crumbled blue cheese

2 tbsp. cream
¼ chopped walnuts

Trim crusts from bread. Butter the bread.

Mix cheese and cream, whipping until smooth. Add chopped nuts and mix well. Spread mixture on bread. Make 3 sandwiches and cut each into quarters.

Serves 3.

PINEAPPLE AND CHEESE SANDWICHES

1 small can crushed pineapple
8 oz. cream cheese, softened
2 tbsp. pineapple preserves

Shredded iceberg lettuce
6 slices light toast

Drain crushed pineapple until all juices are out. Set aside pineapple.

Mix cream cheese and pineapple preserves.

Trim toast. Spread each slice with cream-cheese mixture. On 3 slices, place crushed pineapple and cover with shredded lettuce. Cover with remaining toasts. Cut each sandwich into 4 triangles.

Serves 3.

STRAWBERRY SANDWICHES

4 slices day-old white bread
4 oz. cream cheese
1 tbsp. cream

1 tsp. coarse-ground black pepper
6 large very ripe strawberries

Trim crusts from bread and set aside.

Mix cream cheese with cream to soften. Mix well until smooth, then add black pepper. Mix well until pepper is blended into cream cheese. Spread cheese mixture on all the bread. Slice strawberries and arrange on 2 slices of bread. Cover with remaining bread and cut each into 4 small sandwiches.

Serves 2.

BANANA SANDWICH

In my book, this is the only way to enjoy a banana.

6-in. piece French bread
¼ stick cold butter

1 firm cold banana

Split bread lengthwise.

Slice thin slices of butter over each bread half and spread in a little. Slice banana on bottom bread half and cover with top half. Voila, and enjoy!

Serves 1.

VARIATION

1 tbsp. butter
1 tbsp. mayonnaise
2 small bananas

8 oz. cream cheese, softened
3 tbsp. evaporated milk
6 slices bread

Mix butter and mayonnaise and set aside.

Mash bananas. Whip in cream cheese and milk. Mix well and let chill.

Spread slices of bread with butter mixture. Place cream cheese and banana mixture on bread to make sandwiches. Cut into small pieces.

Serves 3.

Soups and Gumbos

*L*earning from others is fun. It helps you expand the knowledge you already have. It's profitable too because you can often apply that knowledge to business. It's like choosing from a menu. The menu is just somebody's ideas. You have the capacity to use your own imagination and incorporate something else into that menu to create new ideas. I've learned to pick out those ideas and expand on them to make my business a little better. If the ideas don't work, you can always try something else or go back to what you did before. It's surprising where those ideas can come from if you just leave yourself open enough to receive them.

I'd like to talk about the men in my life. By that, I mean the men who have formed clubs and organizations and who have come to my restaurant to meet and eat. I have many favorites because I try to treat each one in a special way.

One group called the Boulé holds meetings here at Dooky's. This is a brainstorming group. I enjoy feeding them because I learn so much from them. For one, they've taught me how to brainstorm ideas more effectively. They're a great bunch of men with interesting ideas to share. I learn something new every time they come.

They originally met at the big hotels, but somewhere in the sixties, two of the members, Dr. Norman Francis and Justice Revius Ortique, decided to give *me* a chance. They've been meeting here ever since. Usually, I'll serve a special surprise for them so they look forward to coming back.

The Boulé never ask me to provide them with a menu in advance. The menu is provided on the table and they see it when they get here. They trust that I'm going to surprise them with something special. The surprise might be a soup, or it may be a special cornbread or side dish. They know I've done that just for them, and they appreciate the effort. It's fun for them. Some of the dishes are as new and interesting as the ideas they bring to share.

It goes back to the idea of giving more than what a customer expects. I believe that whatever you give, you receive twice as much in return.

44

RED LENTIL SOUP WITH HAM

1 lb. red lentils
1 gal. water
½ cup chopped onions
¼ cup chopped celery
½ cup butter-flavored or vegetable
  oil

1 lb. smoked ham, diced
Salt and pepper to taste
½ cup chopped red bell pepper

Wash lentils well and drain. Place lentils in large pot with water. Add onions and celery. Boil for 45 minutes. Lower fire and continue to cook.

Heat oil over a medium fire in a skillet. Cook ham in oil for 10 minutes. Pour ham and oil over lentils. Cook over a low fire for another 30 minutes until lentils are creamy. Salt and pepper to taste. Add red bell pepper. Stir and serve.

Serves 4.

HAM, TOMATO, AND BASIL SOUP

6 large very ripe tomatoes
Boiling water
¼ cup butter-flavored or vegetable
  oil
2 tbsp. flour
½ lb. ham, finely chopped
½ cup finely chopped onions

2 tbsp. tomato paste
2 cloves garlic, chopped
2 tbsp. fresh or 1 tbsp. dried basil
2 qt. water
1 tbsp. Lawry's Seasoned Salt
1 tsp. red pepper flakes

Place tomatoes in boiling water and let sit about 5 minutes. Take tomatoes from water and remove skins, which should be very easy. Discard skins. Put tomatoes in food processor and just barely crush them. Set aside.

Heat oil over a high fire and add flour to make a roux. Brown lightly, about 4 minutes. Add ham and onions and cook until onions are soft, about 5 minutes. Add tomato paste, stirring constantly. Place ham mixture into a large pot. Add tomatoes, garlic, and basil. Add 2 qt. water and let come to a boil. Lower fire and add seasoned salt and pepper. Let simmer for 30 minutes. May be served with corn chips.

Serves 4-6.

BEEF BOWL SOUP

1 lb. beef sirloin
3 qt. water
½ cup soy sauce
1 tsp. cayenne pepper

½ lb. fettuccini noodles
2 hard-boiled eggs, sliced
½ cup chopped green onions

Cut beef in small cubes and place in large pot. Add water, soy sauce, and cayenne. Boil for 35 minutes. Add fettuccini and cook about 10 minutes more. Pour into wide bowl. Place egg slices on top and sprinkle green onions over.

Serves 4-6.

CABBAGE AND BEEF SOUP

1 3-lb. cabbage
1 lb. boneless beef stew meat
1 gal. water
1 large can diced tomatoes
1 medium onion, chopped
1 medium bell pepper, chopped

½ cup chopped celery
1 large carrot, peeled and sliced
2 bay leaves
2 tbsp. Lawry's Seasoned Salt
1 tsp. red pepper flakes

Cut cabbage in small pieces and wash well. Set aside. Cut beef in very small pieces.

Put beef in large pot with water. Add tomatoes, onions, bell pepper, celery, carrots, bay leaves, and red pepper flakes. Bring to boil and cook for 25 minutes. Add seasoned salt and cabbage. Cook until cabbage is just tender, about 10 minutes.

Serves 4-6.

FISH SOUP

1 5-lb. whole redfish or any
   firm-fleshed fish
3 qt. water
1 cup chopped onions
1 cup chopped celery
2 medium carrots, diced
3 bay leaves
2 whole dried red peppers
2 medium white potatoes, cubed
2 sprigs fresh or 1 tsp. dried
   thyme

1 tbsp. paprika
1 tbsp. Lawry's Seasoned Salt
   with Tabasco
1 qt. water
1 cup frozen green peas
½ cup chopped red bell pepper
1 lemon, seeded and thinly sliced
Parsley for garnish

Have fish scaled and all insides removed. Leave head on. Wash fish well inside and out. Put fish in large pan with 3 qt. water. This should cover fish. Add onions, celery, carrots, bay leaves, and dried red peppers. Boil fish for 30 minutes. Remove fish from water, saving the stock, and set fish aside to cool.

Pour fish stock in large pot. Add potatoes, thyme, paprika, and seasoned salt. Add 1 qt. water and let come to a boil. Cook for 5 to 10 minutes until potatoes are just tender. Lower fire.

Remove skin and head from fish. Pull all flesh from bones, picking all meat from head. Break fish in pieces and add to stock. Add peas, bell pepper, and lemon slices. Simmer over a low fire until peas are just tender, about 5 minutes. Remove bay leaves and whole peppers. Sprinkle parsley over soup in bowl.

Serves 4-6.

CRAB SOUP

3 medium blue crabs
½ cup vegetable oil
3 tbsp. all-purpose flour
¾ cup chopped onions
¼ cup chopped celery
½ cup chopped bell pepper
1½ qt. water

1 clove garlic, chopped
1 tsp. whole thyme
½ tsp. cayenne pepper
1 tsp. paprika
1 tbsp. chopped parsley
2 tsp. salt
½ lb. white crab meat

Female crabs are very good for this recipe.

Clean all crabs and cut in halves. Heat oil in a pot over a high fire. Add crabs and fry in hot oil for 10 minutes. Remove crabs and set aside.

Lower fire. To the oil, add the flour, stirring constantly. Cook roux until light brown, about 10 minutes. Add onions and celery and cook over a medium fire until onions are translucent, about 5 minutes. Add bell pepper and cook for about 3 to 4 minutes. Add water, pouring slowly while stirring. Add garlic, thyme, cayenne, paprika, parsley, and salt. Return crabs to liquid; let cook for 30 to 40 minutes. Stir in white crab meat and simmer over a low fire for 5 minutes.

Serves 6.

CORN AND CRAB SOUP

6 ears white or yellow corn
½ cup butter
3 blue crabs, thoroughly cleaned
3 tbsp. flour
½ cup chopped onions
½ cup chopped celery

1 qt. water
1 tbsp. Lawry's Seasoned Salt
½ tsp. cayenne pepper
1 12-oz. can evaporated milk
1 lb. white crab meat

Cut corn off cobs. Place corn kernels in food processor and pulse twice, then set aside.

Melt butter in a large pot over a high fire. Sauté crabs in butter about 5 minutes; do not brown. Remove crabs and set aside.

Turn fire to medium. Add flour to butter, stirring. Add onions and celery and cook for 5 minutes, stirring frequently. Pour in water, stirring as you pour. Return crabs to pot. Let come to a boil and cook for about 10 minutes. Stir in corn, seasoned salt, and cayenne. Lower fire. Add milk and crab meat. Simmer for 30 minutes.

Serves 6-8.

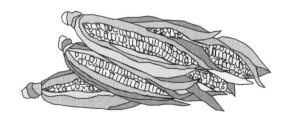

ASPARAGUS SOUP WITH TURKEY BACON

2 lb. fresh asparagus
1 qt. water
½ lb. turkey bacon
3 tbsp. flour

4 cups chicken stock
½ cup chopped green onions with
  bottoms

Wash asparagus and set aside 4 spears. Cut remaining asparagus in pieces. Boil cut asparagus in water until very soft, about 10 minutes.

Cut bacon in 1-in. pieces. Spray a skillet with nonstick cooking spray. Heat over a high fire and add bacon. Cook until crisp, about 5 minutes. Remove bacon.

Turn fire to medium. Add flour to skillet and stir well, cooking 5-6 minutes. Add chicken stock to roux, stirring constantly. Boil about 10 minutes. Add green onions. Add mixture to asparagus and stir well with whisk. Mash asparagus against side of pot and stir well. Let simmer over a low fire for 30 minutes.

Add bacon and remaining asparagus. Cook until asparagus is tender, about 5 minutes.

Serves 4-6.

CREAM OF RED ONION AND POTATO SOUP

4 large white potatoes, peeled and
  quartered
½ cup butter
3 cups diced red onions
1 qt. half-and-half

2 cups milk
1 tsp. salt
1 tsp. white pepper
1 tbsp. chopped chives

In 2-qt. saucepan, boil potatoes in water just to cover until very soft, about 10 minutes. Mash potatoes in the water they are boiled in. Set aside.

In a large skillet, melt butter over a low fire. Add onions and cook until soft, about 5 minutes. Pour into a large pot. Stir in potato mixture. Slowly add half-and-half and milk, stirring constantly. Add salt and pepper. Simmer for 30 minutes. Add chopped chives.

Serves 4-6.

BROCCOLI SOUP

2 whole bunches broccoli
1 gal. water
1 tbsp. salt
1 tsp. white pepper

1 stick butter
4 tbsp. flour
½ cup chopped onions
1 cup chopped celery

Put broccoli in water with salt and pepper. Boil for 40 minutes. Strain broccoli, saving the liquid. Keep liquid hot. Cut off stalks and discard. Chop remaining broccoli.

Melt butter in a large pot over a low fire. Add flour. Stir well. Add onion and celery, stirring, for about 10 minutes. Do not let mixture brown.

Add mixture to liquid. Add broccoli.

Serves 4-6.

SWEET POTATO SOUP

4 large sweet potatoes
1½ qt. water
4 whole cloves
1 tsp. salt
¼ tsp. nutmeg

¼ tsp. cinnamon
1 tbsp. sugar
½ tsp. coarse-ground black pepper
2 tbsp. butter

Peel sweet potatoes and cut in quarters. Put in water with cloves and salt. Boil until potatoes are soft, about 20 minutes.

Drain potatoes, saving the liquid. Blend potatoes in blender. Return to liquid, whisking well.

Add nutmeg, cinnamon, sugar, pepper, and butter. If mixture is too thick, add a little water. Let cook over a medium fire until flavors blend, about 30 minutes.

Serves 4-6.

NAVY-BEAN SOUP WITH CHERRY TOMATOES

1 lb. dried navy beans
4 qt. water
2 bay leaves
½ cup vegetable oil
2 tbsp. flour
1 cup chopped white onions

½ lb. smoked ham, diced
6 cloves garlic, finely chopped
1 qt. water
1 tbsp. salt
1 tsp. white pepper
12 whole cherry tomatoes

Put beans in the 4 qt. water with bay leaves. Boil for about 1 hour, until beans are soft.

In a skillet, heat oil over a low fire. Add flour, stirring about 5 minutes. Do not brown roux. Add onions and ham; stir well and cook about 5 minutes. Add garlic.

Mash beans with whisk. Add ham mixture to mashed beans. Slowly add 1 qt. water. Whip mixture well. Add salt and pepper. Simmer over a low fire for about 30 minutes. Add tomatoes.

Serves 6.

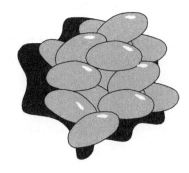

GUMBO Z'HERBES

1 bunch mustard greens
1 bunch collard greens
1 bunch turnips
1 bunch watercress
1 bunch beet tops
1 bunch carrot tops
½ head lettuce
½ head cabbage
1 bunch spinach
2 medium onions, chopped
4 cloves garlic, mashed and
   chopped

Water
1 lb. smoked sausage
1 lb. smoked ham
1 lb. brisket stew meat
1 lb. boneless brisket
1 lb. hot chaurice
5 tbsp. flour
1 tsp. thyme leaves
1 tbsp. salt
1 tsp. cayenne pepper
1 tsp. filé powder
Steamed rice

Clean all vegetables, making sure to pick out bad leaves and rinse away all grit. In a large pot place all greens, onions, and garlic. Cover with water and boil for 30 minutes.

While this is boiling, cut all sausages and meats into bite-size pieces and set aside. Keep chaurice pieces separate.

Strain vegetables after boiling and reserve liquid. In a 12-qt. stockpot, place all meats, except chaurice, and 2 cups reserved liquid, reserving the rest of the liquid. Steam over a high fire for 15 minutes.

While steaming, place chaurice in a skillet over a high fire and steam until chaurice is rendered (all grease cooked out), about 10 minutes. Drain chaurice, keeping the grease in the skillet, and set aside.

All vegetables must be pureed. This can be done in a food processor or by hand in a meat grinder.

Heat the skillet of chaurice grease over a high fire and stir in flour. Cook roux for 5 minutes or until flour is cooked (does not have to brown). Pour roux over meat mixture; stir well.

Add vegetables and 2 qt. reserved liquid. Let simmer over a low fire for 20 minutes. Add chaurice, thyme, salt, and cayenne; stir well. Simmer for 40 minutes. Add filé powder; stir well and remove from fire. Serve over steamed rice.

Serves 8.

CREOLE GUMBO

This is a dish that always preceded any festive meal, or Sunday dinner for that matter. Every woman took pride in her gumbo making. I can remember, as a youngster, the care that went into gumbo making—how the crabs and shrimp were cleaned on Saturday and placed overnight in the icebox.

On Sunday morning, we rose early to attend Mass (in those days, Sunday Mass was in the mornings). Once we were back home, Sunday clothes were taken off and neatly hung up. Hats (as they were a must for women at Mass then) were put back into the armoire. Then, in less formal clothes, it was off to the kitchen. But before the gumbo making began, a cup of coffee and a hot calas (rice doughnut) or a biscuit were served.

Then, every female who was old enough helped prepare the Sunday meal. The aroma of crabs frying filled the house. Chicken necks and gizzards were cleaned and cut up along with sausages, ham, and chicken wings. It seemed that veal stew meat, for whatever reason, was also a must. My job was cutting onions and other seasonings. My mother always made the roux, which took extreme care to get it just right.

4 crabs, cleaned
½ lb. Creole hot sausage, cut in
   bite-size pieces
½ lb. smoked sausage, cut in bite-
   size pieces
½ lb. boneless veal stew meat
½ lb. chicken gizzards
½ cup vegetable oil
4 tbsp. flour
1 cup chopped onion
4 qt. water
6 chicken wings, cut in half

½ lb. chicken necks, skinned and
   cut up
½ lb. smoked ham, cubed
1 lb. shrimp, peeled and deveined
1 tbsp. paprika
1 tsp. salt
3 cloves garlic, finely chopped
¼ cup chopped parsley
1 tsp. ground thyme
2 doz. oysters with liquid
1 tbsp. filé powder
Cooked rice

Put crabs, sausages, stew meat, and gizzards in 6-qt. pot over a medium fire. Cover and let cook in their own fat for 30 minutes (it will be enough, but continue to watch the pot).

Heat oil in a skillet over a high fire and add flour to make a roux. Stir constantly until very brown, about 10 minutes.

Add onions and cook over a low fire until onions wilt, about 5 minutes. Pour onion mixture over ingredients in the large pot.

Slowly add water, stirring constantly. Bring to a boil.

Add chicken wings, necks, ham, shrimp, paprika, salt, garlic, parsley, and thyme. Let simmer over a low fire for 30 minutes.

Add oysters and liquid; cook for 10 minutes longer. Remove from fire. Add filé powder, stirring well. Serve over rice.

Serves 8-10.

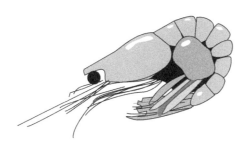

Sauces

Everybody will tell you the same thing, just in different ways. Gen. George Patton, for example, said something to the effect that every man can be famous if he perseveres. Nelson Mandela was the complete opposite of Patton, but by his example we can surely learn what perseverance means. Famous people don't start out with the intention of being famous. Fame becomes a byproduct of people doing what brings them joy. Their joy becomes contagious.

I'll never forget the day I first met the Rev. Dr. Howard Thurman. His joy just radiated outward. He came into the restaurant, smiled at me, and said, "Sister, I want some barbecued ribs, plain and everyday." His words struck a chord in me. Here was an outstanding dignitary from Boston University. I was all set to fix some elaborate meal for him and all he was asking for was a simple pleasure.

I didn't know too much about Dr. Thurman then, but I knew I wanted to know more about this deeply spiritual man. Dr. Johnnetta Cole, who at the time was president of Spelman College, promised to send me something he had said to her students. Since then, I have spent a few minutes every day absorbing his *Inspirational Readings*. His thoughts inspire me to strive harder; they move me to action. He's a fine example of an ordinary man choosing to live his life extraordinarily. That's what good people do, I believe. They touch you in such a way that you want to be better, just for having known them. Sometimes we're not even aware that we have touched somebody so deeply that it has changed the way they live their lives. Simple caring words have the power to do that.

I think God puts people like Dr. Thurman in our lives to give us those messages of love and to show us how to use them. It doesn't matter whether we're famous people or not. What matters is that we get the message and use it to help someone else. That's the miracle. These people affect us in such deep and spiritual ways that it changes how we treat each other, and that helps to change a whole society.

ORANGE MEUNIERE SAUCE

Sauces are not my thing. I never liked anything smothered under too much sauce. However, I will do a few in my kitchen. Here are some of my favorites.

1 cup butter	**2 tbsp. chopped green onions**
½ cup orange juice	**2 tbsp. chopped parsley**
1 tbsp. orange zest	

Cook butter on a low fire until brown, about 10 minutes. Be careful not to burn butter. Slowly stir in orange juice. Add orange zest and stir. Add green onions and parsley. Cook for 5 minutes.

SAUCE BLANCHE (WHITE SAUCE)

This is the first sauce I learned to make, and you can see why. It is so simple. It is great over cauliflower or other boiled vegetables.

1 tbsp. cornstarch	**3 tbsp. water**
¼ tsp. salt	**1 cup milk**
¼ tsp. white pepper	

Mix cornstarch, salt, and pepper. Add water, stirring well.
Bring milk to a boil. Slowly add cornstarch mixture, stirring constantly. Lower fire. Simmer until milk thickens, about 10 minutes.

VARIATION

2 tbsp. butter	**¼ tsp. salt**
2 tbsp. flour	**¼ tsp. white pepper**
1 cup milk	

Melt butter over a medium fire. Blend in flour and cook 6-7 minutes. Slowly add milk. Season with salt and pepper. Stir until smooth, cooking 3-4 minutes.

HOLLANDAISE SAUCE

This sauce can be a little tricky, because if you cook it over a fire that's too high it will separate. If this does happen, slowly add a little warm water and whip it.

6 egg yolks, beaten	¼ tsp. salt
6 tbsp. lemon juice	1 cup butter, softened

Boil water in bottom of double boiler. Place yolks in top of double boiler. Stir in lemon juice. Constantly stirring, add salt. Slowly add butter. Continue to stir until butter is completely melted and mixture is thickened.

Keep over warm water until ready to serve. You can also refrigerate it. When you need it again, just slowly add a little hot water to the refrigerated sauce.

VARIATION

½ cup butter	¼ tsp. Lawry's Seasoned Salt
3 egg yolks	¼ tsp. cayenne pepper
1 tbsp. lemon juice	½ cup boiling water

In a bowl, beat butter until creamy. Add egg yolks one at a time. Beat well. Add lemon juice, seasoned salt, and pepper. Slowly add boiling water.

Place bowl in pot of boiling water or use a double boiler. Stir rapidly until mixture thickens, about 10 minutes. Serve immediately.

BECHAMEL SAUCE

This is a sauce I turn into anything I want just by adding to it. If I want a sauce for pasta, I add my all-time favorite, Romano cheese. For a sauce over vegetables, I add some Herbes de Provence. I also use it for a base for cream soups . . . whatever!

½ cup butter	2 cups evaporated milk
¼ cup finely chopped onion	1 cup water
½ cup flour	Salt and white pepper to taste
1 tbsp. garlic powder	

Melt butter over a low fire. Add onions and cook until clear, about 10 minutes. Add flour, stirring constantly and cooking about 5 minutes. Add garlic powder. Slowly add milk, stirring to avoid lumps. Add water, salt, and pepper. Stir and cook until smooth, about 10 minutes.

If I find that the sauce is a little too thick, I just add a bit more evaporated milk.

You can refrigerate the sauce. When you need it again, just slowly add a little hot water to the refrigerated sauce.

SWEET AND SOUR SAUCE

½ cup light brown sugar	4 tbsp. soy sauce
¼ tsp. cayenne pepper	1 cup pineapple juice
2½ tbsp. cornstarch	1 cup red maraschino cherry juice
½ cup white vinegar	

I like this on baked turkey wings.

In a small bowl, mix sugar, cayenne, and cornstarch. Mix well, making sure cornstarch has no lumps.

Add vinegar and soy sauce, beating to make a smooth paste.

In a saucepot, bring juices to a boil. Add sugar mixture to juices, stirring constantly. Lower fire. Cook until mixture thickens and becomes translucent, about 15 minutes.

BARBECUE SAUCE

A few years ago, I did a job for Lawry's Seasoned Salt at this great barbecue festival called Memphis in May. Well, my dear, you have never seen such a "hoopla" over barbecue. Here in New Orleans, we don't take barbecue too seriously, unless it's barbecued shrimp, which is not barbecue at all. Not so in Memphis. Barbecue is the thing. It is really something to see.

Memphis in May is a great barbecue cookoff. Contestants come from all parts of the country. Their barbecue pits, grills, or whatever they are called are fascinating. Some are so large they are brought in on eighteen-wheelers. Lawry's pit was quite interesting. It was shaped like a giant teapot.

Now I thought the way the meat was prepared was the big thing. Well, no way. I learned it was all about the sauce. I said, "Okay. I'll go down to the grocery and choose the best-looking sauce on the shelf. Kraft—that's a good old reliable brand. You can't go wrong there."

"No, Leah," I was told. "You have to make the sauce yourself."

Okay, a bottle of catsup, Worcestershire, a little mustard, and shake it up . . . barbecue sauce, eh?

Again, I was told, "No, Leah. You have to cook it."

Well, how do you start? Creoles will start any dish with onion, bell pepper, and celery. So here is my . . . *Won't Win a Prize Barbecue Sauce.*

¼ cup vegetable oil
½ cup chopped onions
½ cup chopped bell peppers
½ cup chopped celery
6 cloves garlic, mashed and
  chopped

1 qt. + 2 cups catsup
¼ cup yellow mustard
¼ cup Worcestershire sauce
½ cup Steen's molasses
3 tbsp. Tabasco sauce
2 tbsp. liquid smoke

In a large saucepan, heat the oil over a medium fire. Add the onions, bell peppers, and celery. Cook for 5 minutes until onions are soft. Add garlic and blend well. Stir in catsup, mustard, and Worcestershire sauce. Slowly add molasses and stir well. Add Tabasco and liquid smoke. Let simmer over a low fire for 30 minutes.

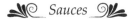

TARTAR SAUCE

1 cup mayonnaise
1 tbsp. dill relish
1 tbsp. chopped capers

1 tsp. horseradish
1 tsp. chopped green onions
¼ tsp. cayenne pepper

Mix all ingredients together. Let chill. Serve on seafood.

CURRANT JELLY SAUCE

2 tbsp. butter
2 tbsp. flour
½ cup chopped celery
2 tbsp. red pepper flakes

2 cups chicken broth
1½ cups currant jelly
2 tbsp. chopped parsley

Melt butter over a medium fire. Add flour and stir constantly until flour browns, about 10 minutes. Lower fire.

Add celery and pepper flakes. Slowly stir in chicken broth. Cook for 15 minutes. Remove from fire and strain.

Add jelly to the strained sauce. Stir in parsley. Simmer over a low fire for 5 minutes. Serve at room temperature.

LEMON SAUCE

Serve this over bread pudding or pound cake.

3 tbsp. butter	1 cup sugar
2 tbsp. flour	1 cup milk
3 tbsp. lemon juice	1 tbsp. grated lemon rind

Melt butter in a pot over a medium fire. Slowly add flour. Stir well and cook about 15 minutes.

Add lemon juice and sugar. Continue to mix. Stir in milk and lemon rind. Whip until smooth. Cook over a low fire about 10 minutes until mixture thickens.

LEMON HARD SAUCE

Serve this no-cook sauce over pudding or pecan pie.

½ cup butter	3 tbsp. lemon juice
2 cups confectioners' sugar	1 tbsp. lemon-flavored vodka

Soften butter. Add sugar. Beat well.

Slowly add lemon juice, beating constantly until mixture is light. Add vodka and beat 2 minutes more.

Chef Leah Chase on the set of her television cooking show, "Creole Cooking with Leah Chase"

The "gold room" at Dooky Chase

The main dining room, which also features some of Mrs. Chase's important art collection

The Victorian Room

Creole Gumbo (see recipe on page 54)

Shrimp Clemenceau (see recipe on page 67)

The daily buffet

Fresh fruit and vegetables adorn the daily buffet

Seafood

It's always best if you know the group that will be dining with you. That way you can set the mood to make their dining a pleasant experience. Running a restaurant is not much different from entertaining at home. Sometimes you entertain the "paper plate" group and sometimes the "get out the good china" group. Sometimes the groups are made up of the same people, but the occasion calls for a change in atmosphere.

At Dooky's, the Bunch Club is a little more relaxed than the Boulé. They have their share of discussions too, but theirs is more of a social gathering. They meet monthly to catch up on the latest around town and enjoy a good meal.

Knowing that, the thing for me to do was come up with an atmosphere and menu suitable for their meetings' style. A buffet was just the thing for them. They could get up and serve themselves whenever there was a break in the meeting. Or they could hold their informal conversations while they selected their food. That way they could enjoy a relaxed meal that fit the mood of the group.

No matter what I put on the buffet, though, I had to have oysters—maybe because oysters are supposed to be brain food. They're also supposed to be an aphrodisiac. I don't know what the members of this group did once they left Dooky's. I just know they enjoyed their meeting and their food while they were here.

SHRIMP CLEMENCEAU

1 stick butter	½ cup sliced button mushrooms
2 medium potatoes, peeled and diced small	1 cup green peas
2 lb. small shrimp, peeled and deveined	¼ tsp. chopped fresh parsley
	⅓ cup white wine
2 cloves garlic, finely chopped	Salt and pepper to taste

Melt butter in a 2-qt. saucepan over a high fire. Add potatoes. Cook 5 minutes.

Add shrimp, garlic, and mushrooms. Cook until shrimp are tender, about 5 minutes. Add peas, parsley, and wine. Salt and pepper to taste. Cook for 5 minutes.

Serves 4.

STEWED SHRIMP

¼ cup vegetable oil	1 tbsp. Lawry's Seasoned Salt
2 tbsp. all-purpose flour	1 tsp. red pepper flakes
½ cup chopped onions	1 tsp. thyme leaves
½ cup chopped celery	2 tbsp. chopped parsley
2 cloves garlic, mashed and chopped	2 large white potatoes, peeled and quartered
2 8-oz. cans tomato sauce	1 lb. shrimp, peeled and deveined
2 cups water	Cooked rice
½ cup diced bell pepper	

In a deep skillet, heat oil over a high fire. Add flour and stir well. Cook flour until just lightly brown, about 6 minutes.

Add onions and celery. Cook until onions are clear, about 5 minutes. Stir in garlic and tomato sauce. Simmer over a low fire about 30 minutes.

Slowly add water, stirring as you pour. Be careful not to leave lumps. Add bell pepper, seasoned salt, pepper, thyme, and parsley. Bring to a boil. Cook for 5 minutes.

Add potatoes and let cook for another 5 minutes. Lower fire and add shrimp. Let simmer until potatoes and shrimp are done, about 10 minutes. Serve over rice.

Serves 4.

DEVILED SHRIMP

1½ lb. shrimp, peeled and
  deveined
Salt and pepper to taste
¼ cup butter
¼ cup flour
¼ cup finely chopped onions
4 hard-boiled eggs

3 cups evaporated milk
1 tbsp. Worcestershire sauce
1 tsp. Louisiana Gold (hot sauce)
2 tbsp. chopped parsley
Breadcrumbs
Paprika

Season shrimp with salt and pepper. Heat butter in a skillet over a medium fire. Add shrimp. Stir until shrimp are just pink, about 4 minutes. Remove shrimp from butter and set aside.

Add flour to hot pan. Stir well so flour will not lump, cooking about 5 minutes. Add onions and continue to stir about 3 minutes.

Put boiled eggs in processor. Chop fine.

Slowly add milk to flour mixture, stirring constantly until mixture is smooth. Add Worcestershire and hot sauce. Add chopped eggs to milk. Toss in shrimp. Cook until shrimp are done, about 5 minutes. Add parsley.

Pour shrimp mixture in ramekins and sprinkle with breadcrumbs and paprika. Brown in oven at 375 degrees about 20 minutes. Serve with toast points.

Serves 4-6.

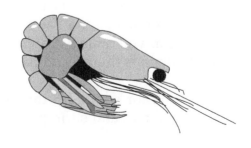

TOMATOES STUFFED WITH
SPINACH AND SHRIMP

½ lb. raw shrimp
3 cups water
1 tsp. Lawry's Seasoned Salt
1 lb. frozen chopped spinach
Bacon for garnish
1 tbsp. butter
6 green onions, chopped

2 cloves garlic, mashed and
    chopped
2 tbsp. Herbsaint
1 tsp. Louisiana Gold (hot sauce)
4 medium ripe tomatoes
½ cup seasoned breadcrumbs

Peel shrimp, saving shells and heads. Devein shrimp, chop, and set aside.

Place shells and heads in water with seasoned salt. Boil for 10 minutes. Drain and save stock. Discard heads and shells.

Place spinach in shrimp stock. Cook over a high fire for 15 minutes. Drain and set aside.

In sauté pan, cook bacon until crisp. Drain bacon on paper towel and set aside.

Add butter to bacon drippings in the sauté pan. Heat pan over a medium fire and add shrimp. Stir in green onions and garlic. Sauté until shrimp pieces are done, about 5 minutes. Add spinach to shrimp mixture. Let simmer over a low fire until well blended, about 15 minutes. Add Herbsaint and hot sauce and stir well.

Cut off stem ends of tomatoes. With a small spoon, remove insides of tomatoes. Use insides for another use. Stuff tomatoes with spinach mixture. Top with breadcrumbs and crumbled bacon. Bake at 400 degrees for 10 minutes.

Serves 4.

MRS. DOMINIQUE'S OYSTER FRICASSEE

We get visitors at Dooky's from all over, but the great ones are those from Louisiana and small towns all over the South. They talk about food and its preparation with all the love in the world.

The Dominique family came to visit from a little town called Gheens, Louisiana. The family was just so warm and wonderful. Mrs. Dominique gave me this great oyster recipe. When you look at it you will wonder about the length of time, but understand, we are never in a hurry when preparing our special dishes. I particularly like the cabbage in this dish. Cook this just as Mrs. Dominique says. It will work and taste great over rice.

1 cup flour	1½ tsp. black pepper
½ cup vegetable oil	1½ tsp. cayenne pepper
½ cup olive oil	1 tbsp. Worcestershire sauce
1 cup chopped celery	2 cups thinly sliced cabbage
1½ cups chopped onion	1 qt. oysters with liquid
1 cup chopped green onion	¼ cup chopped parsley
5 garlic cloves, chopped	¼ cup chopped green-onion tops
2 qt. water	Cooked white rice
2 tsp. salt	

To begin, make roux with flour and oils in a large pot over a medium fire. When dark brown (about 15 minutes), add celery, onions, and garlic. Cook until soft, about 5 minutes, stirring so roux does not stick on bottom of pot. Add water slowly, stirring. Add salt, peppers, and Worcestershire. Cook for 1 hour over a medium-high fire, stirring often.

Then add cabbage and oyster liquid. Cook 30 minutes more. Add parsley, green onions, and oysters to gravy. Simmer over a low fire for about 20 minutes. Taste and add more seasoning to your gravy as needed. Gravy should coat a spoon when fully cooked.

Serve over cooked white rice.

Serves 8.

RED POTATOES STUFFED WITH OYSTERS

I used this recipe for New Orleans' Chef's Charity for Children. It was a great day for me—frightening, but a big challenge. This was my first time being invited to participate in this great fundraiser. Previously, it had been all men. The charity was founded by a chef whom I always admired, Warren Le Ruth, and the other participants were chefs so far greater than I. However, I was able to hold my own with the help of Chef John Folse, who was always egging me on.

6 whole medium red potatoes
2 doz. large oysters with liquid
1 tbsp. butter
¼ cup chopped green onion
4 cloves garlic, mashed and
   chopped

¼ tsp. Lawry's Seasoned Salt
Pepper
Chopped parsley
Breadcrumbs
Paprika

Boil potatoes until just tender, about 15 minutes. Let cool, then cut potatoes in half. Scoop insides out of potatoes and set all aside.

Place oysters in pot in their own liquid. Heat over a medium heat until oysters just curl, about 10 minutes. Drain and save liquid.

Heat butter in a skillet over a low fire. Add onions and garlic and cook about 10 minutes, being careful not to burn.

Chop oysters and add to onion mixture. Stir well. Add liquid from oysters. Cook 5 minutes.

Mash potatoes. Add to oyster mixture. Season with the salt and pepper. Add parsley. Fill potato shells with mixture. Top with breadcrumbs and paprika. Bake at 375 degrees for 10 to 15 minutes.

Serves 3.

BAKED STUFFED RED SNAPPER WITH SHRIMP AND CRABMEAT

1 3-lb. red snapper
Salt to taste
Lawry's Lemon Pepper
½ lb. claw crabmeat
½ cup butter-flavored or vegetable
   oil
½ lb. small shrimp
1 large onion, chopped

½ cup chopped bell pepper
½ cup chopped celery
Cayenne pepper to taste
1 cup seasoned breadcrumbs
Thin onion slices
1 8-oz. can tomato sauce
½ cup water

Scale snapper. Remove insides and eyes. Season fish inside and outside with salt and Lawry's Lemon Pepper. Set aside.

Pick through crabmeat, removing all shell particles. Set aside.

Heat oil in a skillet over a high fire. Chop shrimp and add to oil, stirring well. Add onions, bell peppers, and celery. Season mixture with salt and cayenne. Cook for 10 minutes until onions and shrimp are just tender.

Add crabmeat. Stir mixture well. Tighten with breadcrumbs. Let cool.

Stuff cavity of fish with shrimp and crab mixture. Place fish in well-greased baking pan. Place onion slices over fish. Pour tomato sauce and water over fish. Bake uncovered at 350 degrees for 35 minutes. Fish is done when it flakes.

Serves 4-6.

PECAN-CRUSTED TROUT
WITH ORANGE MEUNIERE SAUCE

1 cup flour	1 egg, beaten
Salt to taste	1 cup milk
½ tsp. paprika	4 8-oz. trout filets
¼ cup finely chopped pecans	½ stick butter

Mix flour, salt, paprika, and pecans in a bowl.

Mix egg with milk.

Dip filets in milk and egg mixture. Dredge in seasoned flour and pecan mixture.

Heat butter in a skillet over a medium fire. Brown filets about 6 minutes on each side. Place on hot platter.

ORANGE MEUNIERE SAUCE

½ stick butter	1 tbsp. chopped parsley
½ cup orange juice	Orange slices for garnish

Heat butter in a skillet over a medium fire. Let brown but do not burn. Add orange juice and parsley and cook about 5 minutes. Pour over fish. Garnish with orange slices.

Serves 4.

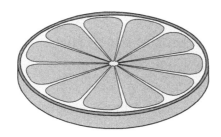

BASS FILETS STUFFED WITH POTATO

3 boiled potatoes
¼ cup chopped onion
¼ cup chopped celery
1 tbsp. chopped garlic

1 tsp. Lawry's Salt Free 17
¼ tsp. cayenne pepper
4 6-oz. bass filets

This recipe is low sodium and low fat.

Peel and mash potatoes. Set aside.

Spray a skillet with nonstick cooking spray. Sauté onions and celery over a medium fire for about 5 minutes. Add garlic and cook 1 minute, being careful not to brown. Add mashed potatoes, Salt Free 17, and cayenne. Cook for 5 minutes.

Lay fish filets on a board. Rub with a little Salt Free 17. Spread each filet with potato mixture. Roll filets up. Place in a baking dish that has been sprayed with nonstick cooking spray. Cover with foil. Bake at 375 degrees for 20 minutes. Uncover and let fish get just a little brown, about 10 more minutes.

Serves 4.

BAKED SEA BASS

4 6-oz. sea bass filets
Salt and pepper to taste
Juice from 1 large lemon
1 stick butter
1 Vidalia onion, thinly sliced

1 red bell pepper, sliced
2 tbsp. chopped parsley
1 can cream of celery soup
½ can cold water

Season filets with salt, pepper, and lemon juice. Place seasoned filets in hot butter over a medium fire. Cook about 5 minutes on each side until barely brown.

Place fish in baking dish. Add onions, sprinkling over fish. Bake at 350 degrees for about 5 minutes.

Add sliced red pepper and 1 tbsp. parsley over fish. Pour celery soup and water over fish, spreading soup mixture evenly. Sprinkle top with remaining parsley. Place in oven and bake at 375 degrees for 15 minutes.

Serves 4.

PAN-FRIED SAC-A-LAIT

Sac-a-lait is white crappie. When Mother went fishing on the bayou, there would be a sac-a-lait in the bunch. There were also other kinds of fish that she called goggle eyes. The meat of the sac-a-lait, when cooked, was very white and had a mild, almost sweet taste.

2 or 3 sac-a-lait
Salt and pepper to taste

Cornmeal or fish fry
2 cups vegetable oil

Scale fish. Remove entrails and eyes. Leave heads on.
Wash fish well. Score fish with knife, making two slits on each side. Season fish well with salt and pepper.
Dredge the whole fish in cornmeal or fish fry. Heat oil over a high fire. Place fish in hot oil for 10 minutes on each side depending on the size of the fish.
Serves 2-3.

COURT-BOUILLON OF SALMON

4 salmon steaks
Salt and pepper to taste
1 stick butter
¼ cup chopped red onions
2 cloves garlic, mashed and chopped

1 cup dry white wine
1 large red bell pepper, diced
½ tsp. dill
1 cup water
1 tbsp. chopped parsley

Season salmon with salt and pepper. Heat butter in a pot over a high fire. Place salmon steaks in hot butter. Cook for about 2 minutes on each side. Remove to warm platter.
Lower fire and add onions and garlic to pot, stirring as you add them. Cook until onions are just soft, about 5 minutes. Add wine, bell pepper, dill, and water. Bring to a boil. Add salmon steaks to liquid. Simmer steaks over a low fire for 5 to 6 minutes. Add parsley. Taste for seasoning.
Serves 4.

POACHED FISH CAKES

4 6-oz. perch filets
½ lb. salmon filet
1 onion, pureed
1 tbsp. chopped parsley
1 tbsp. salt
1 tsp. cayenne pepper
2 eggs, beaten

1 cup flour
2 whole carrots, thickly sliced
2 ribs celery, chopped
2 bay leaves
2 tbsp. liquid crab boil
2 qt. hot water
Mustard

Cut fish in small pieces. Put fish in a food processor and chop very small. Pour fish into bowl and add onions, parsley, salt, and cayenne. Add eggs and mix well.

Dust hands with flour and shape mixture into light, round cakes, covering them well with flour. Dust a cookie sheet with flour and place cakes on sheet. Set in refrigerator for 1 hour until cakes are firm.

In a wide deep pot, place carrots, celery, bay leaves, crab boil, and water. Bring to a rolling boil. Place each cake gently into boiling water. Cook about 5 minutes per side until cakes are done. Serve with mustard.

Serves 4-6.

CREOLE CRAB CAKES

1 lb. lump crabmeat
¼ cup chopped green onions with
  bottoms
1 egg, beaten
2 tbsp. mayonnaise
1 tbsp. Creole mustard

1 tsp. Lawry's Seasoned Salt
1 tbsp. chopped parsley
1 cup breadcrumbs
1 cup butter-flavored or vegetable
  oil

Place crabmeat in a large bowl. Pick through crabmeat, removing all shell particles. Add onions and egg. Toss until egg is mixed thoroughly.

Stir in mayonnaise, mustard, seasoned salt, and parsley. Toss lightly. Let chill for 1 hour in refrigerator.

Pour breadcrumbs in a bowl. Scoop crabmeat mixture (1 tbsp. at a time) into breadcrumbs. Shape into 8 round cakes, squeezing in the breadcrumbs as you shape cakes. Dust cakes well with breadcrumbs.

Heat oil in a skillet over a medium fire. Place crab cakes in hot oil. Brown lightly on each side, cooking about 3 to 4 minutes per side.

Serves 4.

SAUTEED SOFT-SHELL CRABS

To clean a soft-shell crab, lay the crab flat. Raise each side of the upper shell. Pull the shell back halfway. Pull off the soft part under each side of the shell. Pull off the part that flaps under the crab. Pull out the eyes and the bag behind the eyes. Wash the crab thoroughly.

4 soft-shell crabs
Salt and pepper to taste
1 cup flour
½ cup butter-flavored or vegetable
  oil

Juice of ½ lemon
¼ cup water
1 tbsp. chopped parsley

Clean crabs thoroughly. Season with salt and pepper. Dust with flour. Place crabs shell down in hot oil over a high fire. Turn and brown on both sides, about 6 minutes per side. Pour lemon juice over crabs.

Deglaze the pan with water. Remove crabs to platter. Pour liquid over crabs.
Garnish with parsley.

Serves 4.

Meats

I've stirred these pots through many a year,
In times of joy and through many a tear.
It was simple faith that erased my fear.

Ever since I was old enough to remember, I can remember lessons in faith. My mother didn't walk out in faith, she took giant leaps. She was a woman ahead of her time in her thinking. When our church wanted to build a new school, she sold "bricks" to everybody from the insurance man to the mayor. It didn't matter to her that they were of another faith. She just knew that the school had to be built. When the school was up and running, she was its first PTA president.

It's no wonder my faith is strong. I had good role models. I put a whole lot of trust in prayer. When I'm feeling overwhelmed by commitments and I'm not sure which corner is the next one I'm supposed to turn, I say a little prayer. My favorite one is simple: *Divine word of Jesus, I trust in you.*

That always gives me the strength I need to get through the day. It's the one thing I've learned to rely on. You learn quickly in life that *your* agenda is not necessarily anyone else's. Trusting in what you believe is possible will help you succeed. For your business to survive, no matter what the business, you have to realize this lesson early on.

You've got to have a vision, and somewhere in that vision you've got to believe that you can accomplish everything you want. There will be obstacles and disappointments—and sometimes those stumbling blocks come from places and people you least expect—but nothing is impossible if you have faith. Faith will keep you moving in the right direction. It will give you the clarity you need to make those tough decisions, and it will always take you through those times of doubt and fear.

When you finally get to the other side of that obstacle, you're stronger because you were able to survive it. It's like making a tough piece of meat tender. You know the battle you face, but when it's time to eat, you savor the meal because you know what it took to make it tasty.

VEAL CHOPS WITH BUTTON MUSHROOMS

12 button mushrooms
1 tsp. Lawry's Garlic Salt
1 tsp. Lawry's Seasoned Pepper
4 thick veal rib chops
½ stick butter

1 tbsp. flour
½ cup dry red wine
1 cup water
2 tbsp. chopped green onion

Remove stems from mushrooms. Chop stems very fine, leaving mushrooms whole, and set both aside.

Mix garlic salt and seasoned pepper. Rub chops on both sides with the seasoning mixture.

Melt butter over a high fire and place seasoned chops in hot butter. Cook on both sides, being careful not to burn butter. Cook about 5 minutes and remove chops.

Add flour to drippings, stirring and scraping. Slowly add wine. Continue to stir.

Add water. Stir well and bring to a boil. Return chops to pot and add mushrooms and green onions. Cook for 10 minutes and taste and adjust seasoning.

Serves 4.

ROASTED DOUBLE-CUT VEAL CHOPS

1 cup extravirgin olive oil
2 tbsp. chopped garlic
4 8-oz. trimmed double-cut (thick)
   veal chops

Lawry's Steak and Chop Rub
Salt to taste

Preheat oven to 375 degrees.

Mix olive oil with garlic. Lay chops in a baking pan. Pour olive-oil mixture over chops, coating both sides.

Rub chops on each side with Steak and Chop Rub and salt. Bake for 30 minutes, or longer if you like them really well done.

Serves 4.

VEAL A LA MODE

1 tsp. ground thyme
1 tbsp. salt
1 tbsp. black pepper
½ lb. thick bacon
4 cloves garlic, halved
2 tbsp. Herbes de Provence

1 cup water
6 lb. veal rump roast, bone in
3 large white potatoes, peeled and
   quartered
3 large mushrooms, thickly sliced
2 red onions, quartered

Mix thyme, salt, and pepper and set aside. Cut 2 strips of bacon into 4 pieces each; reserve the rest of the bacon. Cut 8 1-in.-long slits throughout roast. In each slit, stuff salt mixture. Stuff a piece of bacon and a piece of garlic in each slit. Rub entire roast with salt, pepper, and Herbes de Provence.

Pour water in bottom of a roasting pan. Put roast in pan and lay remaining strips of bacon over roast, covering with foil. Bake at 350 degrees for 45 minutes to 1 hour.

Uncover roast and baste with drippings. Add potatoes, mushrooms, and onions. Cover and cook for another 25 minutes, until meat and potatoes are done.

Serves 8-10.

VEAL SHANKS WITH TOMATOES AND GARLIC

4 veal shank steaks
Salt and pepper to taste
¼ cup olive oil with garlic
½ cup dry white wine
2 cups water

1 large can plum tomatoes
2 tbsp. garlic, chopped
½ tsp. dried oregano
½ tsp. dried basil
Chopped parsley for garnish

Rub shanks with salt and pepper. If you don't have olive oil with garlic, add 1 mashed clove garlic to ¼ cup olive oil. Heat oil in a skillet over a high fire and place shanks in hot oil, braising about 5 minutes per side. Deglaze pan with wine, scraping the bottom.

Add water and cook for 25 minutes, turning shanks twice. The water and wine should be reduced by half and the meat should be just about tender. Pour tomatoes over meat, breaking them up, and stir in garlic, oregano, and basil. Taste for correct seasoning, cover, and simmer slowly over a low fire for 20 minutes. Sprinkle with chopped parsley.

Serves 4.

COWBOY STEW

We were never told why this was called cowboy stew, unless it was to make this sad dish sound exciting to children who loved cowboys.

4 strips bacon	2 large ripe tomatoes
2 lb. ground beef	Boiling water
2 tbsp. flour	1 cup water
1 red onion, cut in large pieces	Salt and pepper to taste
1 can baby lima beans, undrained	
1 can whole-kernel corn, undrained	

Cook bacon in a heavy skillet over a medium fire until crisp. Remove from skillet and set aside. Add beef to bacon drippings, stirring and breaking up the beef. When brown, sprinkle with flour and cook until flour is well blended, about 10 minutes.

Add onions and cook until soft, about 5 minutes. Add lima beans and corn, including the liquid.

Dip tomatoes in boiling water. Skin tomatoes and squeeze out seeds. Cut tomatoes in small pieces and add to mixture. Crumble bacon and add. Stir well. Add water and let simmer over a low fire for 20 minutes. Season with salt and pepper.

Serves 8.

BARBECUED MEATLOAF

1 lb. ground beef
1 lb. ground pork sausage
½ cup chopped onions
¼ cup diced green bell peppers
1 carrot, peeled and finely
  chopped

1 cup seasoned breadcrumbs
1 egg, beaten
1½ cups barbecue sauce
1 tsp. salt
1 tsp. black pepper

In a mixing bowl, mix beef and sausage well. Add onions, bell pepper, and carrots and stir well. Add breadcrumbs, egg, ½ cup barbecue sauce, salt, and pepper. Mix well until all ingredients are blended.

Shape into loaf and place on a baking pan. Bake at 350 degrees for 35 to 40 minutes. Brush with remaining barbecue sauce. Cook for another 15 minutes and test to see if loaf is cooked through.

Serves 8.

STUFFED BURGERS

4 strips bacon
2 lb. ground beef
1 tsp. Lawry's Seasoned Salt
1 tsp. black pepper
3 tbsp. catsup
1 egg, beaten

½ cup breadcrumbs
8 thin slices red onions
½ cup shredded cheddar
½ cup shredded pepper jack
   cheese
4 toasted hamburger buns

Lay bacon in a hot skillet over a high fire. Cook until very crisp and set aside, saving bacon drippings.

Season ground beef with seasoned salt and pepper. Mix in catsup and egg. Add breadcrumbs and mix well. Make 8 balls of the beef mixture. Pat out on a board, making 8 evenly rounded patties.

Over 4 patties place a slice of onion. Then cover those with cheese. Over each cheese-covered patty, break 1 strip bacon. Cover with remaining 4 patties, mashing sides to seal stuffing in.

Reheat bacon drippings over a medium fire and place stuffed burgers in hot fat. Brown about 4 minutes per side. Add remaining onions and cook until onions are just tender, about 5 minutes. Serve on buns.

Serves 4.

COUNTRY BEEF HASH

2 large white potatoes
2 cups leftover beef gravy
3 cups cubed leftover roast beef,
   including all debris

1 12-oz. can carrots and peas,
   undrained
Cooked rice

Peel and cube potatoes. Boil 10 minutes in water to cover.

Put gravy in a saucepot and heat over a medium fire. Add beef and carrots and peas (including the liquid). Drain potatoes and add them to beef mixture. Let simmer over a low fire for 10 minutes. Serve over rice.

Serves 6.

ROASTED CORNED BEEF WITH RED PEPPER JELLY GLAZE

1 5-lb. corned beef brisket or
  inside round
2 tbsp. sugar

1 tbsp. yellow mustard
2 cups water
1 12-oz. jar red pepper jelly

Preheat oven to 350 degrees.

Leave pickling spices on corned beef. Place beef in a roasting pan. Mix sugar and mustard in water and pour over beef. Cover beef with foil and bake for 45 minutes.

Remove foil. Brush beef with some jelly. Continue to cook covered for 15 minutes or until tender. Brush on jelly several times during the process.

Cool beef and slice across the grain, holding the knife at an angle away from you.

Serves 8-10.

BEEF DAUBE

For this you'll need a good old-fashioned Dutch oven or good Magnalite roaster.

1 tsp. salt
1 tbsp. black pepper
¼ tsp. mace
1 4- to 5-lb. chuck roast
¼ cup flour
¼ cup vegetable oil
2 cups water

1 large onion, cut in 8 wedges
3 cloves garlic, mashed and
  chopped
2 carrots, peeled and cut in 1-in.
  pieces
1 8-oz. can tomato sauce
1 cup water, optional

Mix salt, pepper, and mace and rub roast on all sides with mixture. Pat flour over roast.

Heat oil in a pot over a high fire and place roast in the pot. Brown on all sides. Cover pot and cook roast on very low fire for 15 to 20 minutes, turning often.

Pour water over roast, cover, and continue to cook for 30 minutes.

Remove cover and add onions, garlic, carrots, and tomato sauce. You may need more water at this point. Taste to adjust seasoning. Cook until roast is fork tender, about 20 minutes.

Serves 8-10.

PAN-BROILED STEAK WITH OYSTERS

2 14- to 16-oz. beef T-bone steaks
1 tsp. salt
1 tbsp. coarse-ground black pepper
2 doz. oysters with liquid

½ stick butter
1 tbsp. flour
1 tsp. paprika
2 tbsp. chopped parsley

Rub steaks on both sides with salt and pepper. Heat a large cast-iron skillet that has been sprayed with nonstick cooking spray over a high fire. Place steaks in hot pan and brown on both sides. Use tongs or a spatula, not a fork. You don't want to stick the steaks because they will lose their juice. Lower fire and let steaks cook, turning often, about 12-14 minutes.

Put the oysters and their liquid to boil. When they come to a boil and just begin to curl, take them out of the liquid. Save the liquid and chop half the oysters, leaving half the oysters whole.

In a small skillet, melt butter over a medium fire and stir in flour, mixing well. Cook about 10 minutes. Slowly add oyster liquid and stir well. Pour in chopped oysters, stir, and cook about 2 or 3 minutes. Add whole oysters. Pour over steaks and sprinkle with paprika and parsley. Serve immediately. Serves 2.

BEEF TENDERLOINS WITH DUXELLE OF MUSHROOMS AND HAM

6 6-oz. beef filets
Lawry's Steak and Chop Rub
1 tbsp. butter
½ lb. thinly sliced boiled ham, chopped

½ lb. mushrooms, finely chopped
2 tbsp. chopped green onions
2 tsp. chopped parsley
3 tbsp. cream

Make 2 1-in. slits in sides of each filet. Season filets well with steak rub. Set aside.

Melt butter in a small pan over a medium fire. Add ham and mushrooms. Cook for 5 minutes.

Add green onions and parsley. Mix in cream. Stir well. Remove from fire and let set for a few minutes. Stir well.

Stuff mixture into beef slits. Cook beef on a hot grill until about medium done, about 4 minutes per side.

Serves 6.

HAM STEAK WITH PINEAPPLE

1 tbsp. butter
2 tbsp. brown sugar
¼ tsp. ground cloves
1 tbsp. yellow mustard
1 small can crushed pineapple

1 large center-cut ham steak, about 1½ lb.
½ cup vodka
4 slices pineapple, in juice
Chopped parsley for garnish

Melt butter in a large skillet over a high fire.

Mix sugar, cloves, mustard, and crushed pineapple. Rub ham steak on both sides with mixture. Place ham in hot butter. Cook on both sides, barely browning, about 4 to 5 minutes on each side. Take ham steak from skillet and lay on a warm platter.

Deglaze skillet with vodka. Place pineapple slices in skillet and cook about 3 minutes per side. Add a little pineapple juice.

Pour sauce over ham steak, including pineapple slices. Garnish with chopped parsley.

Serves 3-4.

SMOTHERED PORK CHOPS

This recipe is a nice way to use end-cut pork chops.

3 6-oz. pork chops
Salt and pepper to taste
2 tbsp. flour
½ cup butter-flavored or vegetable
**   oil**

1 cup water
2 onions, sliced
1 green bell pepper, cut in long
**   strips**

Rub chops with salt and pepper and dredge each chop in flour, coating lightly. Heat oil in a large sauté pan over a high fire. Place chops in hot oil and brown about 4 minutes per side. Drain out any excess oil.

Add water and stir bottom of pan. Turn chops over. Bring to a boil, then lower fire and let cook for 5 minutes.

Add onions on top of chops, cover, and cook until onions are just soft, about 10 minutes. Add bell pepper. Season to taste with more salt and pepper and let simmer for 5 minutes longer.

Serves 3.

ROAST LEG OF PORK

2 tbsp. salt
2 tbsp. black pepper
1 leg pork
6 cloves garlic
Salt and pepper to taste
2 tbsp. flour
2 cups water

4 large turnips, peeled and cut in
    1-in. cubes
2 large red onions, cut in large
    pieces
1 small head cabbage, cut in 8
    wedges

Mix salt and pepper together. Make 6 1-in. slits in pork. Rub 2 tbsp. salt and 2 tbsp. pepper in each slit and stuff with garlic.

Rub roast all over with salt and pepper. Dust roast with flour. Place in a roasting pan with water.

Cook uncovered in 400-degree oven for 30 minutes, allowing roast to brown a little.

Cover and lower oven to 350 degrees. Cook for 1½ hours.

Uncover and add turnips and onions. Cook until turnips are just tender, about 15 minutes.

Add cabbage. Cook for 15 minutes longer.

When pork is done, slice thin. Place vegetables on a platter around pork. Serves 8.

GREAT BALLS OF PORK

These go well with mashed sweet potatoes.

2 lb. ground pork
1 medium white onion, chopped
1 cup cracker meal
2 eggs, beaten
1 tbsp. Lawry's Seasoned Salt
1 tsp. white pepper
1 cup breadcrumbs
1 cup butter-flavored or vegetable
   oil

½ cup golden raisins
1 Granny Smith apple, peeled,
   cored, and chopped
½ cup dried apples
2 cups apple juice
½ cup Steen's molasses
½ cup apple jelly

In a large bowl, mix pork, onions, cracker meal, eggs, seasoned salt, and pepper. Shape mixture into 6 balls. Roll balls in breadcrumbs.

Heat oil in a skillet over a high fire. Brown balls lightly on all sides, about 5 minutes.

Remove balls from skillet. Place in a baking dish. Sprinkle raisins and apples around balls. Pour apple juice and molasses over all. Bake at 375 degrees for 15 minutes.

Remove baking dish from oven and brush balls with apple jelly. Return to oven and cook for 10 minutes more.

Serves 6.

LAMB PATTIES WITH ROSEMARY AND OKRA

2 lb. boneless lamb roast, ground
2 tbsp. chopped green onions
   with bottoms
1 tbsp. chopped parsley
2 tbsp. chopped garlic
1 tbsp. Lawry's Seasoned Salt
1 tsp. black pepper
1 egg, beaten
½ cup heavy cream

1 cup flour
½ cup butter-flavored or vegetable
   oil
8 oz. diced tomatoes
1 tbsp. fresh rosemary
1 10-oz. pkg. frozen cut okra
1 cup water
Salt and cayenne pepper to taste

Mix lamb with onions, parsley, 1 tbsp. garlic, seasoned salt, pepper, egg, and cream. Shape into 6 patties. Roll each patty in flour, shaping patty well.

Heat oil in a skillet over a high fire. Brown patties on both sides. Remove meat from skillet. Set aside.

Lower fire. Scrape bottom of skillet, loosening drippings. Add remaining garlic to skillet. Stir well and cook 1 minute.

Add tomatoes, rosemary, and okra. Pour water over mixture. Season with salt and cayenne. Return patties to skillet. Simmer until meat and okra are just done, about 10 minutes.

Serves 6.

LAMB CHOPS WITH PEARS AND MINT SAUCE

2 pears	2 tbsp. flour
1 tbsp. dried mint leaves	½ stick butter
4 thick lamb chops	½ cup water
Salt and pepper to taste	1 tbsp. mint jelly

Peel pears and remove seeds. Slice thickly and set aside.

Pound mint into a powder.

Season chops with salt and pepper. Rub powdered mint on chops and dredge lightly in flour. Melt butter in a skillet over a medium fire. When butter is just hot, place chops in hot butter and brown lightly on both sides for 5 minutes. Be careful that butter doesn't burn. Chops must not cook too long.

Add pears to skillet around chops. Stir gently. Add water and mint jelly and cook until pears are barely soft, about 6 minutes. Chops should be medium rare to medium.

Serves 4.

LAMB STEW

¼ cup vegetable oil or bacon fat	2 turnips, peeled and cubed
2 lb. boneless lamb stew meat	2 small red potatoes, quartered
Salt and pepper to taste	2 carrots, peeled and cut in ½-in.
2 tbsp. flour	pieces
8 pearl onions or shallots	1 8-oz. can tomato puree
1 tsp. thyme leaves	1 qt. water
1 bay leaf	3 cloves garlic, chopped

Heat oil in a heavy pot over a high fire. Place lamb in pot and sprinkle with salt and pepper. Brown meat.

Sprinkle flour over meat, mix well, and let flour cook, about 5 minutes. Add onions, thyme, bay leaf, turnips, potatoes, carrots, and tomato puree. Pour in water and garlic and let cook over a medium fire about 30 minutes.

Serves 6.

OXTAIL STEW

I wish more people would try this dish. I enjoy preparing oxtail. Sometimes when you can get one large whole one, it is great boned out and stuffed with spicy greens. Here is a stew recipe for oxtail.

½ cup vegetable oil
2 lb. cut-up oxtail
3 cups beef consommé
2 cups water
3 tbsp. flour
1 cup chopped onions
3 cloves garlic, chopped
1 cup dry red wine

2 carrots, peeled and sliced
1 bay leaf
2 sprigs fresh thyme
2 whole dried red peppers
1 12-oz. can sliced mushrooms
¼ cup chopped green onion
Salt to taste

Heat oil in a heavy skillet over a high fire. Brown oxtails on all sides, then transfer them to a large pot. Reserve drippings in skillet. Pour consommé and 1 cup water over oxtails and bring to a boil. Lower fire and let oxtails cook for 1 hour.

In the skillet over a medium fire, brown flour in the oxtail drippings, about 10 minutes. Add onions and garlic. Cook about 5 minutes until onions are just soft.

Deglaze skillet with wine, stirring well. Add carrots and remaining water. Pour this mixture over oxtails, stirring as you pour. Add bay leaf, fresh thyme, and dried peppers that have been broken in 2 or 3 pieces. Add mushrooms, green onion, and salt. Let cook for 30 minutes over a low fire.

Serves 6.

Poultry and Game

If you keep hanging on to yesterday,
you'll never see daylight breaking tomorrow.

$\mathscr{L}$ooking at the past is not a bad thing, but looking at the present to determine where you want to be in the future is the best thing. The black legend of baseball, Satchel Paige, said it right when he said, "Don't look back. Somebody might be gainin' on ya." In business as well as in family affairs, striving to make things better for tomorrow is the best thing you can do for yourself and for those who will come behind you.

It's one of my reasons for doing this book. I want to see those who will be the next generation of entrepreneurs have it better than I did. If somebody else can benefit from the know-how I've gained, then that makes my work worthwhile. Of course, the mainstays are always there. Hard work, patience, and diligence are the ingredients that will make tomorrow better.

I'm scared for today's generation, though. Each generation thinks they've had it harder than the one before. I believe that each generation is burdened with different challenges. For example, in my generation, there was a lack of money but not of morals. In society today, there is a lack of morals but not of money. In some respects, I had it a lot easier than many people growing up today.

That's why I believe that family is so important. The things you learn from family are the building blocks for whom you will become as an adult. I'm very old-fashioned when it comes to family. The role of Momma is irreplaceable. Momma is the glue that keeps family together. She's the one who sets the example of how family members should treat each other.

The first five years of a child's life are so important for learning the basics, and I believe it's Momma who teaches those best, because she's had more practice and patience at doing it.

Some of the most memorable things in my life are our family gatherings. Our family, as large as it is, still gathers to celebrate each other. It's a tradition for us to celebrate everything that comes down the pike.

The family reunion is the biggest event of the year. Our families have grown so large that we have to rent a place big enough to hold all of us.

Then there's the Easter celebration in Lacombe, Louisiana, at my brother's place. That gathering is not as large as the family reunions, but we always manage to get a good crowd there. We all bring food and the children have an Easter-egg hunt. My sister Adonicia is usually in charge of that, even though she doesn't have any small children. She does it because she enjoys seeing the little people having a good time. She also has a piñata filled with toys and goodies for the children. This is what keeps you young, and at the same time it shows children they're important.

As busy as the Christmas season is, the brothers and sisters and their spouses gather on the Saturday before Christmas.

Between those three big events are many others. It might be a graduation party, birthday party, bridal shower, or spur-of-the-moment idea on someone's part.

We *know* how to do parties and picnics. At the family reunion, the pots and dishes are lined up on tables that stretch to kingdom come. It's always amazing to me that we rarely have the same two dishes. Each person old enough to cook has a favorite recipe that is prepared for the reunion. It's mighty awesome to see that many people sharing their lives with each other.

Each time, we have to try something that everyone can participate in. We'll have something like a "crazy hat" contest. We don't have anything outstanding for prizes, just ribbons. The fun is seeing who can come up with the best ideas. Usually, the personalities show themselves in these contests. For the crazy hat contest, my sister Grace decorated her hat with poker chips, cards, and pictures of slot machines. In some former life, she must have been a Mississippi riverboat gambler.

The good thing about having a large family is that you don't have to go too far to find the things you need to put on an affair of that size. Everything is built in. This family has a wide range of talents and professions, from musicians to architects and everything in between. We could start our own village if we had a mind to.

For now, though, we're content with just gathering to celebrate family. Here are some poultry and game recipes that can be enjoyed at any celebration.

ROSEMARY CHICKEN

2 tbsp. Lawry's Seasoned Salt
1 tbsp. white pepper
1 tsp. garlic powder
4 large white potatoes

1 fryer chicken, 3 to 4 lb., cut in 8
  pieces
4 oz. butter, melted
2 tbsp. fresh rosemary

Mix seasoned salt, pepper, and garlic powder in a small bowl.

Peel potatoes and cut in cubes. Let soak in water to cover.

Wash chicken, pat dry, and season with half the salt and pepper mixture.

Spray an ovenproof skillet with nonstick cooking spray. Place chicken in skillet. Rub chicken with butter. Bake at 350 degrees for 30 minutes.

Drain potatoes. Sprinkle with remaining seasoning. Place potatoes over chicken and sprinkle with rosemary. Continue to bake for 30 minutes longer until chicken and potatoes are cooked.

Serves 4-6.

BROILED CHICKEN WITH HERBES DE PROVENCE

2 broiler chickens, 2 lb. each,
  halved
1 tbsp. salt
1 tsp. coarse-ground black pepper

2 tbsp. butter, softened
1 cup white wine
2 tbsp. Herbes de Provence

Season chicken with salt and pepper and rub butter over chicken. Cook chicken inside up under broiler for 20 minutes. Turn chicken over and broil 15 minutes.

Drizzle wine over chicken and sprinkle with Herbes de Provence. Broil another 15 minutes until nice and brown and cooked all the way through.

Serves 8.

CHICKEN AND BASIL

6 4-oz. boneless skinless chicken
  breasts
Salt and pepper to taste
1 stick butter

2 tbsp. flour
1 cup water
1 cup evaporated milk
2 tbsp. chopped fresh basil

Pound chicken breasts lightly. Season with salt and pepper. Heat half the butter in a pan over a high fire and place chicken in hot butter. Lightly brown on both sides, then remove chicken from pan to a plate and set aside.

Put remaining butter in a skillet, melt completely, and stir in flour. Cook about 5 minutes. Whisk well and do not brown flour. Add water and slowly add milk. Stirring, add basil and continue to cook for a few minutes. Place chicken in sauce and let simmer over a low fire for 10 minutes.

Serves 6.

PANEED CHICKEN

6 4-oz. boneless skinless chicken
  breasts
Salt and white pepper to taste
½ cup cream
2 eggs, beaten

½ cup water
1 tsp. paprika
2 cups breadcrumbs
1 cup vegetable oil

Pound chicken breasts lightly. Season with salt and pepper.

In a bowl, mix cream and eggs well. Add water. Place chicken in milk mixture.

Mix paprika with breadcrumbs. Take chicken from milk and press chicken in crumbs, covering well.

Heat oil over a high fire. Place chicken in hot oil and cook until brown on both sides, about 5 minutes per side. Drain chicken on a paper towel.

Serves 6.

LEMON CHICKEN

3 large lemons
2 cups water
1 tbsp. light brown sugar
½ tsp. paprika
4 4- to 6-oz. boneless skinless
  chicken breasts

Lawry's Seasoned Salt to taste
Lawry's Lemon Pepper to taste
½ cup butter
2 cloves garlic, mashed and
  chopped
1 tbsp. chopped parsley

Zest 2 lemons (this is just the thin yellow skin—none of the white rind). Set zest aside.

Squeeze the 2 lemons and set juice aside. Discard remains.

Cut 1 lemon in 4 to 6 thin slices. Boil lemon slices for a few minutes in water. Remove from water (keep the water). Place lemon slices in a small pan and sprinkle with brown sugar and paprika. Set aside.

Season chicken breasts with seasoned salt and lemon pepper. Heat butter in a skillet over a high fire. Add chicken to hot butter, lightly browning on each side.

Add the garlic while stirring the chicken. Be careful not to burn. Add lemon zest.

Pour lemon juice over all. Cook over a low fire about 5 minutes. Add the water that the lemons were boiled in. Let cook until chicken is done, about 5 minutes.

Serve on a plate. Place a lemon slice on each breast. Sprinkle with parsley. Serves 4.

CHICKEN IN CREAM SAUCE

1 tbsp. Lawry's Seasoned Salt
1 tsp. garlic salt
1 tbsp. white pepper
2 fryer chickens
2 cups milk
2 cups flour

2 cups vegetable oil
½ cup cream
3 eggs, beaten
1 tbsp. chopped parsley
¼ cup bacon pieces

Mix seasoned salt, garlic salt, and pepper.

Cut chickens in quarters and remove backbones. Season chickens with seasoned-salt mixture. Pour 1 cup milk over chickens. Remove chickens and dredge each piece in flour.

Heat oil in a heavy skillet over a medium fire and brown chickens on all sides. Place chickens in a baking pan. Mix remaining milk, cream, eggs, and parsley. Pour over chickens. Sprinkle on bacon pieces. Cover with foil, and bake at 375 degrees for 45 minutes.

Serves 8.

CHIPPER CHICKEN

Fish filets can be prepared in this same way.

1 fryer chicken, 3 to 4 lb., cut in 8
   pieces
Salt and white pepper to taste

1 large bag potato chips
1 stick butter

Wash chicken well and pat dry. Season with salt and pepper. Set aside.

Crumble chips and spread on a baking sheet.

Melt butter. Pour over chicken, coating all pieces. Roll buttered chicken in crumbled chips.

Place chicken in a shallow baking pan. Bake at 350 degrees for 45 minutes to 1 hour.

Serves 4.

CHICKEN AND BABY LIMA BEANS

1 cup butter-flavored or vegetable oil
1 fryer chicken, 2½ lb., cut in 8 pieces
½ cup chopped onions
¼ cup chopped celery

2 lb. frozen baby lima beans
¼ cup chopped green bell pepper
1 tsp. chopped garlic
1 qt. chicken stock
Salt and pepper to taste
Cooked rice

Heat oil in a large pot over a high fire. Fry chicken until light brown on all sides, about 10 minutes. Take chicken out of pot and set aside.

Turn fire to medium. Stir in onions and celery and cook about 5 minutes. Then add lima beans, bell peppers, garlic, and chicken stock. Return chicken to pot and let simmer over a low fire until beans and chicken are cooked, about 30 minutes. Taste and adjust seasoning. Serve with rice.

Serves 4.

CHICKEN CACCIATORE

1 fryer chicken, 3 lb., cut in serving pieces
1 tbsp. salt
1 tsp. black pepper
Flour for dredging
½ cup extravirgin olive oil
1 cup water
1 large onion, sliced

5 cloves garlic, chopped
1 large can whole tomatoes
1 tsp. oregano
1 cup sliced mushrooms
2 large green bell peppers, cut in strips
1 tbsp. chopped parsley

Season chicken with salt and pepper. Dredge chicken in flour, covering well. Heat olive oil in a heavy pot over a high fire and brown chicken on all sides.

Lower fire and add water, deglazing the bottom of the pot. Let simmer for 5 minutes. Add onions, garlic, tomatoes, oregano, and mushrooms. Cover and let simmer for 45 minutes.

Add bell pepper and let cook, covered, another 15 minutes until chicken is tender. Season to taste with salt and pepper and finally add parsley.

Serves 4.

STUFFED LEG QUARTERS
WITH BAKED BEANS

This recipe was inspired by that great Lawry's team at the Memphis in May festival. I like Bush's beans for this.

4 chicken leg quarters	½ cup breadcrumbs
1 tbsp. Lawry's Seasoned Salt	1 12-oz. can barbecued baked
1 tbsp. Lawry's Poultry and Pork	beans
Rub	¼ cup molasses or cane syrup

Remove thigh bones from chicken, leaving drumstick intact. Season chicken with seasoned salt and poultry rub.

Add breadcrumbs to 1 cup beans in a bowl, mixing well. Spoon bean mixture onto open chicken thighs. Close with skewers.

Place stuffed legs in a well-greased baking pan. Rub molasses over chicken. Bake at 350 degrees for 30 minutes.

Pour remaining beans over chicken, cover with foil, and cook for another 30 minutes. Remove foil and test for doneness.

Serves 4.

CHICKEN POT PIE

1 chicken, 4 lb.
2 large white potatoes, peeled
2 onions, chopped
2 cups sliced celery
2 bay leaves
1 tsp. salt
1 tsp. cayenne pepper
½ lb. bacon

3 tbsp. flour
1 tbsp. chopped garlic
3 cups chicken broth
3 10-in. piecrusts
½ cup diced cooked carrots
½ cup frozen green peas, thawed
1 tbsp. chopped parsley

Boil chicken with potatoes, onions, celery, bay leaves, salt, and cayenne about 10 minutes. Remove potatoes when they are barely soft and set them aside. Continue cooking chicken until it is tender but not falling off the bone, about 30 minutes.

Cook bacon until crisp. Drain on paper towel and save bacon drippings. Add flour to hot bacon drippings and stir well over a high fire until flour is blended but not browned, about 5 minutes. Add garlic and cook 1 minute.

Add chicken broth, stirring well until mixture is smooth. Season to taste. Let simmer over a low fire until sauce thickens, about 5 minutes.

Pull chicken from bones, discarding all skin. Cut chicken in little pieces and dice partially cooked potatoes.

Take piecrusts from their pans and flatten dough on a board. Cut some dough to fit 4 6-oz. ramekins, reserving rest of dough. Line each ramekin with dough and place chicken in each. Divide potatoes, carrots, and peas among the ramekins. Crumble bacon over each, sprinkle parsley over each, and pour sauce over the top.

Cover with remaining dough, fitting edges tightly. Prick the top dough a few times with a fork. Bake at 375 degrees until brown, about 20 minutes.

Serves 4-6.

CHICKEN LIVERS EN BROCHETTE

1 cup evaporated milk
½ cup water
1 egg, beaten
12 chicken livers

Salt and pepper to taste
6 strips bacon
1 cup seasoned breadcrumbs
2 cups vegetable oil

Mix milk, water, and egg in a bowl. Season livers with salt and pepper. Cut bacon strips in half. Lay bacon strips on a cutting board. Place a liver on each strip of bacon. Roll liver in bacon, securing with a toothpick.

Dip bacon-wrapped livers in milk mixture. Then roll them in breadcrumbs, coating them well. Heat oil over a high fire and fry livers until they are done, about 5 minutes. Drain on paper towel.

Serves 4.

CHICKEN LIVERS WITH CURRANT JELLY SAUCE

1 lb. chicken livers
Salt and pepper to taste
1 cup evaporated milk
½ cup water

1 egg, beaten
1 cup flour
2 cups vegetable oil
Currant Jelly Sauce (see index)

Clean chicken livers. Season with salt and pepper.

Mix milk, water, and egg in a bowl. Dust chicken livers lightly in flour. Dip livers in milk mixture. Shake them well in remaining flour.

Heat oil in a 1-qt. heavy pot over a high fire. Drop livers in hot oil carefully (livers may pop in the hot oil). Turn over, browning on all sides. Cook for 5 to 6 minutes. Serve with Currant Jelly Sauce.

Serves 4.

ROASTED HEN WITH
DRIED FRUIT AND RAISINS

1 hen, 5 to 6 lb.
¼ tsp. ground ginger
1 tbsp. salt

1 tbsp. white pepper
6 oz. bag dried mixed fruit
1 cup chicken broth

Wash hen. Mix ginger, salt, and pepper and rub hen inside and out with mixture. Place dried fruit in cavity of hen and tie legs together with cord.

Place hen in a baking pan and pour chicken broth over hen. Roast at 450 degrees for 30 minutes. Then cover with foil and roast for about 45-60 minutes, until hen is brown and tender.

While hen is roasting, prepare sauce.

RAISIN SAUCE

¼ stick butter
¼ cup chopped onions
1 large carrot, chopped
1 tbsp. flour
2 cups chicken broth

1 cup dark raisins
Hot water
¼ tsp. ground cloves
1 egg yolk, beaten

Heat butter in a saucepan over a medium fire and add onions and carrots. Cook until onions are lightly brown, about 5 minutes. Sprinkle flour over onion mixture and cook about 5 minutes, stirring constantly.

Slowly add chicken broth. Stir well and cook about 10 minutes.

Soak raisins in water for 5 minutes. Drain and add raisins to sauce. Add cloves.

When hen is done, remove from oven. Add drippings to raisin sauce. Beat egg yolk slowly into raisin sauce. Serve sauce over hen.

Serves 10.

STUFFED BAKED HEN

1 baking hen, 6 lb., with neck, gizzard, and liver
3 strips bacon
6 slices stale bread
1 cup milk
½ lb. cooked ham, chopped
1 cup chopped onions
½ cup chopped celery

2 eggs, beaten
¼ tsp. red pepper flakes
½ tsp. dried thyme leaves
3 cloves garlic, mashed and chopped
Salt and black pepper to taste
4 cups water
1 cup port wine

Boil neck, gizzard, and liver in a small pot of water to cover for 30 minutes. Drain and pull meat from neck. Chop meat along with gizzard and liver and set aside.

Cook bacon in a skillet until crisp and remove from skillet. Reserve drippings. When cool, crumble bacon.

Soak bread in a bowl with milk. Mash well until it becomes a soft pulp.

Cook ham, onions, celery, and chopped hen parts in bacon drippings over a medium fire until onions are clear, about 5 to 10 minutes. Add bread mixture and bacon and stir. Mix in eggs, red pepper flakes, thyme, and garlic. Add salt to taste. Cook for 10 minutes, stirring to blend all ingredients. Let cool.

Season hen inside and out with salt and pepper. Stuff with bread mixture. Truss opening with skewers and tie legs together with cord.

Place hen in a heavy pot (like a Dutch oven). Pour water and wine over hen. Boil on stove for 20 minutes.

Then bake in pot at 350 degrees for 1 hour, covered. Baste hen and test for tenderness. Raise temperature to 375 degrees, uncover, and cook about 20 minutes to let brown.

Serves 10.

TURKEY AND SWEET POTATO CASSEROLE

No matter how many guests you have, there is always turkey left over. Here is one way to make a second meal.

6 large baked sweet potatoes
½ tsp. cinnamon
¼ tsp. nutmeg
1 tsp. Lawry's Seasoned Salt

4 cups chopped turkey meat
Leftover turkey gravy
6 strips uncooked bacon

Peel and mash potatoes with cinnamon, nutmeg, and seasoned salt. Spray a Pyrex baking dish with nonstick cooking spray. Spread a layer of mashed potatoes in the dish. Then put a layer of turkey meat over the potatoes. Continue to layer, making sure potatoes are the top layer. Pour a little turkey gravy over the top and lay bacon over the mixture. Bake at 400 degrees until bacon is crisp, about 30 minutes.

Serves 6.

DUCK BREAST WITH ORANGE MARMALADE GLAZE

4 whole boneless duck breasts
  with skin
Salt and pepper to taste

8 1-in.-thick slices French bread
12-oz. jar orange marmalade
Fresh mint leaves

Remove skin from duck and reserve. Cut breasts in half. Season breasts well with salt and pepper. Set aside.

Strip duck skin in thin strips. Place in small skillet and cook over a medium fire until all fat is out, about 15 minutes. Skin should then be nicely browned and crackling. Remove from fat and drain on paper towel.

Place breasts in the hot fat. Brown lightly on both sides. Let cook for about 10 minutes until tender. Remove from fat. Set aside and let cool.

Brown bread slices in the hot fat. Remove from pan and let cool.

Slice duck diagonally in thin slices. Place on fried bread. Using a pastry brush, brush half the marmalade thickly over duck and bread. Bake in a preheated 400-degree oven for 10 minutes. Brush on remaining marmalade and bake 5 minutes more, until duck is well glazed.

Garnish plate with duck cracklings and mint leaves.

Serves 8 as an appetizer.

COUNTRY DUCKLING WITH RICE

1 duckling, 4 to 5 lb.
2 tbsp. salt
2 tbsp. black pepper
1 lemon
1 small onion
2 ribs celery

2 bay leaves
3 sprigs fresh thyme
2 whole cloves
1 tbsp. Herbes de Provence
½ cup melted butter

Clean duckling thoroughly. Mix salt and pepper and rub duckling inside and out with mixture. Cut lemon in half and squeeze lemon over the inside and outside of the duckling. Place onion and celery in duckling cavity and close cavity with a skewer.

Place duckling in a large pot of water (to cover), and add bay leaves, thyme, cloves, and Herbes de Provence. Bring duckling to a boil. Lower fire and cook slowly for 1 hour until duckling is tender.

When duckling is finished, remove from water and save the stock. Place duckling in a baking pan and brush with butter. Bake at 350 degrees until duckling is nice and brown, about 35-40 minutes.

RICE

3 tbsp. fat from duckling stock
2 cups long-grain rice

3½ cups duckling stock
2 tbsp. chopped parsley

Put fat in a heavy 2-qt. pot and heat over a high fire. Stir in rice. Stir well and let rice brown a little. Add stock and parsley. Cover tightly and cook over a low fire until rice is cooked, about 35 minutes.

GRAVY

½ cup melted butter
4 tbsp. flour

Remaining duckling stock

Place butter in a pot over a medium fire and add flour. Stirring constantly, cook until brown, about 10 minutes. Slowly pour stock over roux and whisk over the fire until smooth, about 10 minutes.

To assemble dish, place the rice on a platter. Place duckling on top. Pour gravy around outer edge of platter.

Serves 8-10.

Vegetables and Rices

Whether you're young or growed up,
If ya give up, you're blowed up.
     —Charles Lange, Sr. (my father)

At times the world seems so small, but when trials come your way, it's easy to believe you don't have a friend in the world. It's not until after those special people have crossed your path that you realize they were purposely put there to help you, to lend support.

Once, when I had received a really bad review, I thought my world would come crashing down. Kind words from people on the fringes of my life came to my rescue. One of those people was Ella Brennan. Her words helped me to see that I had to believe things could be better and then make it so. That helped me to keep going on. I knew I could grow from that experience.

Over the years, my pots, too, have become my friends. They allow me to think and dream. As I'm stirring and adding ingredients into that pot, I'm thinking about what will come next in this kitchen or in that dining room— or in my life. I spend long hours on my feet, and some days, all I can see are my pots. So I take refuge there. The pots don't care if I'm laughing or crying. They just sit there waiting for me to fill them.

I think every cook has a favorite pot or pan to make certain dishes. The hand just automatically reaches for that certain pot or pan for that particular dish. My sister Jan makes fried rice in one special skillet that was given to her by our aunt Lucy. Jan says the rice just doesn't taste the same when it's cooked in anything else. She knows that skillet. I know what she's talking about. I'm at home with my pots.

COUNTRY MASHED POTATOES

½ lb. bacon
10 medium red potatoes
1 tbsp. Lawry's Seasoned Salt

1 tsp. Lawry's Seasoned Pepper
2 tbsp. chopped green onions
1 tbsp. chopped parsley

Fry bacon until crispy. Drain on paper towel. Save bacon fat. Set aside.

Wash potatoes well. Do not peel. Boil potatoes whole until fork tender, about 20 minutes.

Slice potatoes in a mixing bowl. Mash potatoes with fork. Potatoes can be a little chunky.

Add 3 tbsp. bacon fat. Season with seasoned salt and pepper. Crumble bacon and add to the potatoes. Mix well.

Add onions and parsley. Mix well. Serve warm.

Serves 6.

GARLIC MASHED POTATOES

6 medium white potatoes
Boiling salted water
6 cloves garlic, mashed and
   chopped

½ tsp. white pepper
1 stick butter
½ cup milk
¼ cup sour cream

Peel and quarter potatoes. Boil in water with garlic until potatoes are very soft, about 15 minutes. Drain potatoes.

Place in a mixer while hot. Whip on medium speed. Add pepper, butter, milk, and sour cream. Mix until fluffy.

Serves 6.

CARROT SOUFFLE

I go to a grocery in a great Creole community. There I'll meet some people I haven't seen in a long time, while others I see often. Creoles' main topic of conversation is food. They can give you all sorts of ideas about food preparation. One suggestion was, "Leah, you should do a carrot soufflé. I had it at a local cafeteria, but I know that you can do a better one." Well, here is my idea of a carrot soufflé.

3 eggs
3 tbsp. butter
3 tbsp. flour
1 cup half-and-half
12 large carrots, peeled, cooked,
   and mashed

¼ tsp. nutmeg
¼ tsp. salt
¼ tsp. white pepper
½ cup breadcrumbs
Melted butter for topping

Separate egg yolks and whites. Beat egg yolks. Set aside.

Melt 3 tbsp. butter in a saucepan over a medium fire. Add flour, stirring well. Cook slowly about 5 minutes; do not brown.

Pour half-and-half into the flour, stirring as you pour. Cook over a low fire about 5 minutes.

Remove from fire. Stir in egg yolks. Mix well.

Stir in carrots, nutmeg, salt, and pepper. Mixture should be thick and creamy.

Beat the egg whites until stiff. Pour into carrot mixture.

Pour carrot mixture into a well-greased baking dish. Sprinkle top with breadcrumbs. Drizzle melted butter over crumbs. Bake at 350 degrees for 30 minutes.

Serves 6.

CARROT PUDDINGS

I prefer these puddings to the soufflé. They are great with lamb chops. For this recipe, I like to steam the carrots. They have less water, making firmer puddings.

10 large whole carrots, peeled and
    washed
½ tsp. Lawry's Seasoned Salt
½ tsp. white pepper

3 tbsp. pureed onions
3 eggs, beaten
½ cup evaporated milk

Steam carrots until tender. Mash carrots well (this should give you about 3 cups). Season with seasoned salt and pepper.

Stir in onions and eggs. Add the milk and whip until smooth.

Spray 4 custard cups or ramekins with nonstick cooking spray. Pour mixture in cups, just a little over halfway up. Place cups in a pan with 1 in. hot water. Bake at 350 degrees for 30 minutes until puddings are set. Test by inserting a knife in centers. If knife comes out clean, puddings are ready. Let cool. Turn out on plate. Serve with Mint Sauce.

MINT SAUCE

2 tbsp. butter
2 tbsp. flour
2 cups cream
2 eggs, beaten

½ tsp. salt
¼ tsp. cayenne pepper
½ tsp. garlic powder
1 tbsp. chopped mint leaves

Melt butter over a medium fire and add flour. Stirring well, cook about 5 minutes, but do not brown. Slowly add cream, continuing to stir. Stir in eggs. Cook about 10 minutes. Mixture should be smooth and not too thick.

Add salt, cayenne, and garlic powder. Taste for seasoning. Stir in mint. Serve over Carrot Puddings.

Serves 4.

GRILLED ASPARAGUS WITH BACON

16 large asparagus spears   8 slices bacon, cut in half
Boiling water

Cut about 1 in. from the bottom of each asparagus. Discard bottoms. Place spears in water and let sit off fire for 2 minutes. Remove from water. Let cool.

Wrap each spear with bacon. Cook on a hot grill until bacon is done, about 10 minutes.

Serves 8.

SAUTEED PEPPER MEDLEY

This is great with chops or grilled chicken.

2 red bell peppers   1 jalapeño pepper
2 green bell peppers   ½ cup butter-flavored or vegetable
2 yellow bell peppers   oil

Cut peppers in half and remove all seeds. Slice peppers in long strips. Wash and drain.

Heat oil over a medium fire. Place peppers in hot oil. Shake and toss lightly. Cook for 5 minutes. Drain and turn peppers out on a hot platter.

Serves 4.

STUFFED LETTUCE WEDGES

Today iceberg lettuce is not very popular. I still love its crispiness when it's really cold, especially served this way.

1 head iceberg lettuce   3 tbsp. half-and-half
8 oz. blue cheese   ½ cup chopped pecans
4 oz. cream cheese

Core lettuce. Cut lettuce in 6 wedges. Wash lettuce gently, taking care not to separate leaves. Let drain.

Mix cheeses with half-and-half until smooth. Add pecans.

With a small spatula, spread cheese mixture between lettuce leaves, keeping wedges intact. Chill and serve with a blue cheese dressing.

Serves 6.

CABBAGE CASSEROLE

1 4-lb. cabbage
1 large onion, quartered
2 whole dried red peppers
1 tbsp. Lawry's Seasoned Salt
1 bay leaf
1 tsp. thyme leaves
3 tbsp. butter-flavored or vegetable
 oil

3 tbsp. flour
1 cup evaporated milk
1 egg, beaten
1½ cups grated Romano cheese
¼ cup breadcrumbs

Remove all bad leaves from cabbage. Cut cabbage in quarters. Remove hard core.

Put cabbage in a large pot with onion, peppers, seasoned salt, bay leaf, and thyme. Cover with water. Boil cabbage for 15 minutes. Strain cabbage. Save liquid.

Heat oil in a skillet over a low fire. Stir in flour. Cook for 5 minutes. Do not brown.

Slowly add 1 cup liquid from cabbage. Add milk, stirring constantly. Stir in egg. Cook for 4 or 5 minutes. Stir well to avoid lumps.

In a casserole dish, place half the cabbage leaves. Pour half the sauce over cabbage. Sprinkle with half the cheese. Then layer on remaining cabbage, sauce, and cheese. Cover casserole with breadcrumbs. Bake at 400 degrees until crumbs are slightly brown, about 15 minutes.

Serves 8.

BROCCOLI CASSEROLE

2 cups shredded cheddar cheese
1 can cream of mushroom soup
½ cup chopped green onions
2 1-lb. pkg. frozen broccoli,
    thawed

¼ stick butter
2 cups crumbled Ritz crackers

Mix cheese, soup, and green onions. Set aside.

Place broccoli in a greased Pyrex baking dish. Spread soup mixture over broccoli.

Melt butter and mix with cracker crumbs. Spread crumb mixture over broccoli. Bake at 350 degrees for 30 minutes.

Serves 8.

BROCCOLI AMANDINE

2 bunches broccoli
Boiling salted water
½ cup butter
¼ cup slivered almonds

1 tsp. coarse-ground black pepper
Juice of 1 lemon
Lemon slices for garnish

Wash broccoli and cut off hard stems. Boil broccoli whole in water 5 to 7 minutes. Drain, place on a dish, and keep warm.

Heat butter over a medium fire. Add almonds. Cook for 10 minutes. Stir in pepper and lemon juice. Pour over broccoli. Garnish with lemon slices.

Serves 6.

BROCCOLI AND PENNE PASTA

1 lb. penne pasta
2 10-oz. pkg frozen broccoli flow-
    erets
1 tbsp. salt
Boiling water
½ cup butter-flavored or vegetable
    oil
2 tbsp. flour

1 12-oz. can evaporated milk
2 cloves garlic, mashed and
    chopped
1 egg, beaten
1 tbsp. Worcestershire sauce
6 large mushrooms, sliced
1 cup grated parmesan cheese

Place pasta, broccoli, and salt in water. Cook until pasta is just tender, about 8 minutes. Drain. Do not rinse. Set aside.

In a skillet, heat oil over a medium fire. Add flour. Stir well and cook about 5 minutes.

Slowly add milk and continue to stir. Cook about 5 minutes. Add garlic.

Add a little of the milk mixture to egg. Beat well. Add egg slowly to the rest of the milk mixture.

Add Worcestershire sauce and mushrooms. Mix well and cook about 3 minutes. Stir in half the cheese. Toss gently with pasta and broccoli. Sprinkle top with remaining cheese.

Serves 6.

BROCCOLI FROSCHIAS

I learn so much from different people. I am truly grateful to them. Each year in Madisonville, Louisiana, on the feast of Saint Joseph, March 19, my sister Cleo and the women in the parish make a beautiful altar in honor of this great saint. They prepare all sorts of food to place on the altar. One thing they prepare I love—called Froschias. They are really little omelets made with a variety of vegetables, my favorite being broccoli. I like these with a little pepper jelly.

3 eggs	**Boiling water**
1 level tbsp. flour	**3 tbsp. olive oil**
1 tsp. Lawry's Seasoned Salt	**4 cloves garlic**
½ tsp. white pepper	**3 tbsp. Romano cheese**
1 bunch broccoli	

Beat eggs well. Add flour, stirring well so flour doesn't lump. Add the seasoned salt and pepper. Beat well. Set aside.

Cut broccoli flowerets from stem. Boil flowerets in water for 5 minutes. Drain and chop.

Heat oil over a medium fire. Slice garlic and add to hot oil, stirring. Cook until garlic is soft, about 2 minutes. Remove garlic from oil. Mash and chop finely. Add garlic to egg mixture. Mix in broccoli and cheese. Mix well.

Drop tablespoonfuls of egg mixture in the hot olive oil. Cook about 3 minutes per side. (They will look like half-dollar pancakes.)

Serves 4.

BROCCOLI SALAD WITH WALNUTS

2 bunches broccoli
Boiling water
1 large red onion, thinly sliced
½ cup chopped walnuts

¼ cup mayonnaise
1 tbsp. Dijon mustard
2 tbsp. balsamic vinegar

Cut broccoli flowerets from stems. Boil flowerets in water for 5 minutes. Remove and drain. Let cool.

Toss onions with broccoli. Add walnuts, mayonnaise, mustard, and vinegar. Toss well. Let chill.

Serves 6.

CAESAR SALAD

2 cloves garlic
2 heads romaine lettuce
2 eggs
2 cups extravirgin olive oil
½ cup red-wine vinegar
Juice of 1 lemon

2 tbsp. Creole mustard
½ cup grated parmesan cheese
Salt and black pepper to taste
Croutons
1 can flat anchovies

Mash garlic. Rub inside of a bowl well with garlic. Discard garlic.

Wash and break lettuce in small pieces. Shake in a strainer to dry. Place lettuce in garlic-rubbed bowl. Cover with plastic wrap. Refrigerate for ½ hour.

Break eggs in a bowl. Beat well. Slowly add olive oil and continue to beat.

Add vinegar and lemon juice. Continue to beat. Add mustard and half the cheese. Beat until creamy. Add salt and pepper.

Pour over chilled lettuce. Toss well, but gently. Top with croutons, remaining cheese, and anchovies.

Serves 8-10.

SALADE FATIGUEE

When lettuce was a few days old but still good, Mother prepared what she called Salade Fatiguée. Also, if this salad is allowed to sit for a while, one can see why it is called *fatiguée* or "tired." The heat from the bacon fat makes the lettuce wilt.

6 strips bacon	**2 hard-boiled eggs, mashed**
1 head iceberg lettuce	**¼ cup vinegar**
1 red onion, finely chopped	

Fry bacon until crisp. Drain and save bacon fat. Cool and crumble bacon. Set aside.

Core lettuce. Wash and drain lettuce. Cut lettuce in small pieces. Place in a salad bowl.

Reheat bacon fat over a medium fire. Put onions in hot fat and cook until soft (about 3 minutes). Stir in eggs. Whisk well until creamy. Add vinegar.

Pour hot mixture over lettuce. Toss well. Sprinkle bacon crumbs over lettuce.

Serves 6.

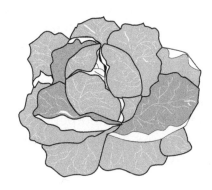

GRILLED VEGETABLES ON WHOLE-WHEAT BUNS

1 small eggplant
Salted water
1 white onion
1 partially green tomato
1 red bell pepper
3 tbsp. olive oil

1 tsp. dried thyme leaves
2 whole-wheat buns, split
Kosher dill pickle sticks
Salt and black pepper to taste
2 tbsp. balsamic vinegar

Peel eggplant and slice thickly. Soak slices in water for 10 minutes.

Slice onion and tomato thickly and set aside.

Cut bell pepper in wide strips and set aside.

Drain eggplant and pat dry with paper towel.

Mix olive oil with thyme.

Toast buns on a hot grill or in a heavy skillet. Garnish with pickles. Brush on olive oil and thyme mixture.

Place eggplant and onion on grill. Sprinkle with salt and pepper. Grill about 3 minutes until eggplant and onion are just soft, then turn once.

Place tomatoes and bell peppers on grill for about 1-2 minutes, turn, and cook for 1-2 minutes.

Sprinkle vinegar over all vegetables. Arrange on wheat buns.

Serves 4.

RED-BEAN LOAF

This makes an excellent meatless main dish.

2 cups cooked drained red beans
2 tbsp. finely chopped onions
1 tbsp. chopped green bell pepper
2 cloves garlic, mashed and
  chopped

1 tbsp. Lawry's Seasoned Salt
1 cup seasoned breadcrumbs
1 tbsp. Tabasco sauce
2 tbsp. barbecue sauce

Combine all ingredients and mix well. Shape into a loaf on a baking sheet or place in a well-greased loaf pan. Bake at 375 degrees for 30 minutes.
Serves 4.

MOCK SAUSAGE PATTIES

1 lb. dried field peas
1 large onion, chopped
3 cloves garlic, chopped
½ tsp. ground thyme

Salt and black pepper to taste
4 eggs
Breadcrumbs
¼ cup vegetable oil

Pick through peas and wash well. Place peas in a pot and cover with water.

Add onions, garlic, and thyme. Bring to boil, then lower fire to medium. Cook peas until tender, about 40 minutes. Drain and mash peas.

Add salt and pepper. Add 2 eggs and mix well. Chill for 1 hour.

Shape mixture into patties. Dredge in breadcrumbs, then in 2 beaten eggs, then again in crumbs. Heat oil in a skillet over a medium fire. Fry patties in hot oil about 5 minutes per side until brown. Drain on paper towel.
Serves 4-6.

GROUNDNUT CROQUETTES

3 cups plain shelled peanuts
2 tbsp. water
2 tbsp. sesame oil
2 tbsp. vegetable oil
2 eggs, beaten
1 tsp. garlic powder

1 tsp. onion powder
1 tbsp. chopped parsley
1 tsp. Lawry's Seasoned Salt
Breadcrumbs
2 eggs, beaten
¼ cup peanut or vegetable oil

Heat peanuts in oven at 350 degrees until warm—5 minutes at most. Place them in a food processor with water and make a paste. Place in a bowl.

Add sesame oil, 2 tbsp. vegetable oil, 2 eggs, and seasonings. Mix well. Shape into croquettes.

Roll in crumbs, then in 2 beaten eggs, then again in crumbs. Heat oil over a medium fire. Fry croquettes in hot oil about 3 minutes per side until brown. Drain on paper towel.

Serves 6.

ZESTY STUFFED EGGS

Cut eggs in half lengthwise. Scoop out and mash yolks. Set aside.

12 hard-boiled eggs
⅓ cup olive oil
⅓ cup evaporated milk
3 eggs, beaten
⅓ cup vinegar
1 tsp. yellow mustard

1 tsp. well-drained dill relish
1 tbsp. hot sauce
1 tbsp. Lawry's Seasoned Salt
Lettuce leaves
Sliced tomatoes

Whisk together olive oil, milk, and beaten eggs. Slowly add vinegar. Cook over a low fire, stirring constantly, until mixture thickens, about 3 minutes.

Add mashed egg yolks to mixture. Whisk until smooth. Add mustard, relish, hot sauce, and seasoned salt. Let cool.

Stuff in hollowed egg whites. Serve on lettuce with sliced tomatoes.

Serves 6.

FRIED PICKLES

3 large whole dill pickles
2 tbsp. water
½ cup evaporated milk

1 egg, beaten
1 cup yellow cornmeal
¼ cup vegetable oil

Slice pickles lengthwise into 5 to 6 slices per pickle. Set aside.
Mix water and milk. Mix in egg.
Dip pickle slices well in milk mixture. Dredge in cornmeal, coating well on all sides. Heat oil over a high fire. Fry slices in hot oil, about 1 minute per side. Drain on paper towel.

Serves 3.

PEAR RELISH

Aunt Tilly always served this with breaded veal.

12 cooking pears
1 cup chopped red bell peppers
1 red onion, chopped
2 cups sugar

¼ cup vinegar
2 tbsp. yellow mustard
1 tbsp. red pepper flakes

Peel and core pears. Chop in small cubes. Place pears in a pot with remaining ingredients. Cook over a medium fire for 30 minutes until pears are just tender.

Serves 12.

RICE SALAD MOLD

This may be served with cold meats such as beef or turkey.

4 cups cooked rice
½ cup seeded chopped tomatoes
¼ cup chopped green bell peppers
½ cup chopped celery
6 pimento-stuffed green olives, sliced
6 pitted black olives, sliced
½ tsp. turmeric

1 tsp. white pepper
2 tbsp. chopped parsley
¼ cup mayonnaise
2 tbsp. yellow mustard
2 envelopes powdered gelatin
2 cups water
Lettuce leaves

In a large bowl, mix rice, tomatoes, bell peppers, celery, and olives. Toss well. Sprinkle in turmeric, pepper, and parsley. Fold in mayonnaise and mustard. Set aside.

Place gelatin in a small pot. Pour in water. Stir well until gelatin is thoroughly dissolved. Cook over a medium fire for 3 minutes.

Pour over rice mixture. Stir well. Spray a mold well with nonstick cooking spray. Pour mixture into mold. Refrigerate for 4 hours or overnight. Turn onto lettuce leaves.

Serves 8.

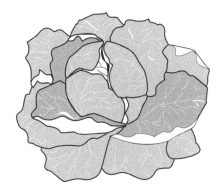

SPICY RICE

1 tbsp. butter
2 tbsp. chopped green bell pepper
2 tbsp. chopped green onion
⅓ cup diced cooked carrots

1 tsp. red pepper flakes
2 cups cooked rice
1 tsp. Lawry's Seasoned Salt
1 tbsp. chopped parsley

Heat butter in a saucepan over a medium fire. Add bell pepper and green onions. Stir to coat peppers well with butter. Cook about 3 minutes.

Add carrots and red pepper flakes. Stir in cooked rice. Add seasoned salt and parsley. Serve hot.

Serves 4-6.

LEMON DILL RICE

2 cups long-grain rice
¼ cup lemon juice
1 tsp. lemon zest

½ tsp. dried or chopped fresh dill
1 tsp. Lawry's Seasoned Salt
3 cups water

Place rice, lemon juice, lemon zest, dill, and seasoned salt in a saucepan. Stir well. Add water and stir.

Cover tightly. Bring to a boil. Cook for 5 minutes. Lower fire and let cook slowly until rice is done (30 minutes).

Serves 4-6.

ISLAND RICE

This is excellent served with grilled pork or chicken.

½ stick butter
½ cup chopped green onions
¼ cup chopped celery
2 cloves garlic, finely chopped
2 cups converted rice
1 cup chopped ripe tomatoes
¼ cup sliced black olives
¼ cup sliced green olives

4 whole cloves
2 bay leaves
½ tsp. thyme leaves
½ tsp. red pepper flakes
1 tsp. salt
1 cup coconut milk
1 tsp. chopped parsley
2 cups water

In a 2-qt. saucepan, melt butter over a medium fire. Add green onions, celery, and garlic. Cook for 5 minutes.

Stir in rice. Mix well and cook for 3 to 4 minutes. Add all other ingredients. Stir well. Cover pan and cook over a low fire for 30 to 35 minutes or until rice is tender. Uncover pan and toss rice lightly.

Serves 6.

VEGGIE JAMBALAYA

2 tbsp. butter
3 cups brown rice
1 cup broccoli flowerets
½ cup diced carrots
¼ cup frozen green peas
2 tbsp. chopped green bell pepper

2 tbsp. chopped red onion
Salt to taste
1 tsp. red pepper flakes
5 cups water
1 tbsp. chopped parsley

Melt butter in a heavy saucepan over a medium fire. Add rice and stir until coated with butter. Add broccoli, carrots, peas, bell pepper, red onion, salt, and pepper.

Pour in water. Stir and bring to a boil. Cover tightly. Lower fire and cook for 40 to 45 minutes. When rice is done, toss in the parsley.

Serves 6.

CORN OYSTERS

6 ears corn
3 eggs, separated
3 tbsp. flour
3 tbsp. vegetable oil

1 tbsp. cream
1 tsp. salt
1 tsp. white pepper
1 cup vegetable oil

Remove all silk from corn and wash corn. Grate corn on coarse side of a grater. Set aside.

Beat egg yolks and whites separately. Add to the corn. Mix in flour, oil, cream, salt, and pepper. Mix well.

Heat oil in a deep pot over a high fire. Drop spoonfuls of batter in hot oil. Fry about 5 minutes, turning frequently, until light brown.

Serves 6.

YELLOW HOMINY

Hominy was one cereal I truly hated. As I remember, it was always white, and it was served with milk and sugar. Creoles called it "Saccamite." Now I've learned there is yellow hominy. It looks better—nice big yellow kernels. I decided to try it, thinking if it looks good, it will taste good. So I tried this recipe and served it with Ham Steak with Pineapple (see index).

2 cans yellow hominy
2 whole large ripe tomatoes
Boiling water
3 tbsp. butter
¼ cup diced green bell peppers

½ cup chopped green onions
1 tbsp. Lawry's Seasoned Salt
1 tbsp. Tabasco sauce
1 tsp. Herbes de Provence

Drain hominy and set aside. Dip tomatoes in boiling water for 5 minutes to remove skins. Peel thin skins from tomatoes. Cut tomatoes in large pieces and set aside.

Melt butter in a saucepan over a medium fire. Add hominy. Cook in butter for a few minutes.

Add tomatoes, bell peppers, and green onions. Let cook slowly for 10 minutes. Add seasoned salt, Tabasco, and Herbes de Provence. Cook for another 5 minutes.

Serves 4-6.

Desserts

Cooking is like an art. You can use your creativity to concoct new dishes anytime the mood strikes you. The pot becomes your canvas and the ingredients you use can result in a masterpiece. It's not a hard thing to do. You just have to be patient and keep testing the ideas. Lord knows, you can always find somebody willing to be your taste tester.

The same thing is true for bringing new ideas to how people eat. Brainstorming is fun, and the rewards are worth it. It's good to think of new and exciting possibilities on a regular basis. When I thought about doing something different at Dooky Chase's, one of the ideas I came up with was a Creole Feast.

I knew that people in New Orleans like to eat for a long time. I can remember growing up the same way. We would sit at the table, eat several courses, and enjoy the conversation, food, and drink for hours. I decided to do a seven- to eight-course meal at the restaurant.

At first, some of our diners didn't fully understand. For the Creole Feast, you have to be prepared to spend at least two hours sitting, eating, and drinking. It was created to have people come and enjoy. I don't like going to a restaurant and having waiters or waitresses rushing you to finish before you've even had a chance to warm the seat you're sitting in.

Everything had to be just so for this feast. We paid attention to details. Sometimes the littlest things make the biggest impression. For one of those events, we were serving sorbet. We put the sorbet spoons in the freezer. It didn't take a whole lot of time to do that, but when the dessert was served, people noticed the coldness of the spoons and how it added to the flavor of the sorbet.

It might be a special garnish or how you set the napkins up. It might be a favor beside the plate, something that diners can take with them as a keepsake of the occasion. It's that little extra touch that brings people back and makes them want to spread the word. Ninety percent of our diners come here through word of mouth.

Community activities will also bring people to you. You just have to be willing to be involved with the things that happen in the community. At the same time, you have to know how to balance your commitments, so that you're sharing your energy and time in the places that will be most beneficial.

I have some women's groups that come to Dooky's for luncheons and an occasional evening meal. The women in these groups are usually more experienced in life. They are still young in mind and spirit even if they've stopped counting their actual ages. They don't grow old, they just grow gracefully.

These women know how to enjoy life. I watch them come in to Dooky's and it seems as though the whole place lights up. They know how to celebrate life, and so I prepare the kinds of food that help them do just that. I might fix something sassy for their dessert. Something like my Bailey's Irish Cream Custard Cake is just spunky enough to end their meal on a note to match their spirits.

LEMON CHESS PIE

After twenty-six years in the air force, my sister Eula's husband, Carol, retired. They settled in Atwater, a small town in Northern California. I visited for the first time not long ago. I was thrilled just looking at all the beautiful orchards of walnut, almond, peach, and lemon trees.

The lemons fascinated me the most. There were lemon trees in the backyards. They were so beautiful and so large. They produced the juiciest lemons I've ever had and they made the best lemonade. Seeing all these lemons made me wonder what wonderful dishes I could create from them.

2 cups sugar
1 tbsp. cornmeal
1 tbsp. flour
4 eggs, slightly beaten
¼ cup milk

¼ cup lemon juice
Grated rind of 1 lemon
¼ cup melted butter
1 9-in. pie shell

Here is a lemon classic.

Mix sugar, cornmeal, and flour. Add eggs, stirring well. Slowly add milk. Continue to mix.

Add lemon juice and rind. Mix in butter. Pour into unbaked pie shell. Bake at 375 degrees for 45 minutes.

Serves 6.

NICE AND EASY LEMON CHESS PIE

1 cup sugar
1 tbsp. yellow cornmeal
1 tbsp. all-purpose flour
½ stick butter, softened

4 eggs, beaten
½ cup lemon juice
½ cup evaporated milk
1 9-in. pie shell

Mix dry ingredients in bowl. Stir in butter. Beat mixture well.
Slowly add eggs and lemon juice. Stir in milk. Mix well.
Pour into unbaked pie shell. Bake at 350 degrees for 1 hour.

Serves 6.

PRUNE PIE

2 cups chopped pitted prunes
2 tbsp. flour
½ cup sugar
1 9-in. pie shell
3 eggs

¼ cup heavy cream
½ cup Oreo cookie crumbs
¼ cup confectioners' sugar
¼ tsp. vanilla extract

Preheat oven to 450 degrees.

In a bowl, toss prunes with flour and 2 tbsp. sugar, coating prunes well. Place in unbaked pie shell. Bake for 10 minutes. Remove from oven. Lower temperature to 350 degrees.

Separate eggs. Set whites aside. Beat egg yolks with remaining sugar.

Add cream and cookie crumbs. Pour mixture over prunes—do not stir. Return to oven, and bake until mixture is set, about 30 minutes.

Beat egg whites until stiff. Slowly add confectioners' sugar and vanilla. Beat again until egg whites peak.

Spread over pie. Return to oven. Bake at 375 degrees until meringue is just tan, about 10 minutes.

Serves 6.

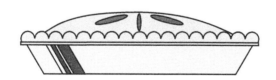

DOUBLE-CRUST PRUNE PIE

2 cups all-purpose flour   1 cup shortening
1 tsp. salt   ¼ cup cold water

Mix flour and salt. Mix in shortening until flour and shortening are like beads. Slowly add cold water.

Work dough with your hands until you have a stiff paste. Make 2 balls of dough. Place in refrigerator about 30 minutes.

Remove dough. Roll 1 ball on a floured board until very thin. Fit it into a 9-in. pie pan, working it up sides of pan. Roll out second ball of dough and set aside.

FILLING

2 cups pitted prunes   1 tsp. cinnamon
1 cup sugar   ½ cup chopped pecans
Juice of 1 lemon   1 tbsp. butter
2 tbsp. cornstarch   1 egg, beaten

Put prunes in water to cover and bring to a boil. Add sugar and lemon juice, and boil until prunes are soft, about 5 minutes. Put cornstarch in ¼ cup water. Stir well, removing all lumps slowly. Add cornstarch to prune mixture. Cook until mixture thickens, about 5 minutes.

Add cinnamon, stirring constantly. Stir in pecans and butter. Mixture should be thick. Let cool to room temperature.

Pour into pie shell. Cover with remaining pie dough. Wet edges and pinch together. Cut small slits in top crust. Brush crust with egg. Bake at 350 degrees for 35 to 40 minutes until pie is nice and light brown.

Serves 6.

SWEET POTATO PIE

4 large sweet potatoes, boiled and peeled	1 tsp. cinnamon
1 cup sugar	½ cup condensed milk
	¼ cup melted butter

Mash sweet potatoes. Add sugar and cinnamon. Mix well.

Whip in condensed milk and butter. Whip mixture until smooth. Set aside.

CRUST

1 cup all-purpose flour	5 tbsp. shortening
1 tsp. salt	½ cup cold water
¼ cup chopped pecans	Cinnamon

Sift flour and salt. Add pecans. Mix in shortening until it is in small lumps. Slowly add water. Mix into stiff paste.

Roll out on a floured board. Fit into an 8-in. pie pan, working it up sides of pan. Prick bottom dough with a fork.

Bake at 450 degrees for a few minutes until crust is barely cooked. Remove from oven. Lower temperature to 350 degrees.

Put sweet potato mixture in crust. Sprinkle top lightly with cinnamon. Return to oven and bake for 35 minutes.

Serves 6.

GEORGE WASHINGTON PIE

1 9-in. pie shell   3 cups Cool Whip
1 can cherry pie filling

   Bake pie shell according to package instructions. Let cool. Gently mix pie filling with 1 cup Cool Whip. Fill pie shell with cherry mixture. Top with remaining Cool Whip. Refrigerate overnight.

Serves 6.

CHERRIES JUBILEE

2 cans pitted Bing cherries   ¼ cup cherry-flavored brandy
2 tbsp. cornstarch   ¼ cup Remy Martin
3 tbsp. water   Vanilla ice cream

   Drain juice from cherries. Place juice in a pot over a low fire. Mix cornstarch well with water. Slowly add to juice, stirring well.
   Add cherry brandy to pot. Stir and continue to cook until mixture thickens a little, about 5 minutes. Add cherries to syrup. Simmer for 5 minutes.
   Pour Remy Martin in a large spoon. Light with a match. Slowly mix burning brandy with cherries. Serve over ice cream.

Serves 4.

BAILEY'S IRISH CREAM CHIFFON PIE

1 tbsp. powdered gelatin	3 eggs, separated
½ cup + 3 tbsp. Bailey's Irish Cream	½ cup brewed coffee
⅓ cup + 2 tbsp. sugar	1 9-in. pie shell
¼ tsp. cinnamon	Whipped cream

In top of a double boiler, mix gelatin with 3 tbsp. Bailey's Irish Cream. Let sit for about 3 minutes. Mix in ⅓ cup sugar and the cinnamon. Beat well.

Add egg yolks and continue to beat. Slowly, add coffee and remaining Bailey's Irish Cream. Make sure mixture is well blended.

Place over boiling water and cook, stirring constantly, until mixture thickens enough to make a thick coating on a spoon, about 10 minutes. Remove from fire and place in refrigerator until cold.

Beat egg whites until stiff. Add remaining sugar and continue to beat until stiff. Fold into cold Bailey's Irish Cream mixture.

Fill pie shell. Chill until set. Top with whipped cream.

Serves 6.

BAILEY'S IRISH CREAM TARTS

2 cups self-rising flour, sifted	8 oz. cream cheese
2 tbsp. cocoa powder	¼ cup softened butter

Mix flour and cocoa. Add cream cheese and butter. Work all ingredients together well. Chill for 30 minutes.

Remove from refrigerator and return to room temperature. Break off balls of dough and press into 24 small muffin tins. Set aside.

FILLING

1 cup firmly packed brown sugar	1 tsp. butter, softened
1 cup chopped pecans	2 tbsp. Bailey's Irish Cream

Mix all ingredients together, making sure the butter is well blended. Using a teaspoon, spoon mixture into tarts. Bake at 350 degrees for 30 minutes or until tarts can be removed from the tins.

Makes 24.

BAILEY'S IRISH CREAM CUSTARD CAKE

1½ cups cake flour
1 tsp. baking soda
½ tsp. salt
3 eggs, slightly beaten

1 cup sugar
2 tbsp. Bailey's Irish Cream
½ tsp. vanilla extract

Preheat oven to 350 degrees.

Mix flour, baking soda, and salt. Set aside.

Place eggs and sugar in a mixing bowl. Beat on medium speed for about 3 minutes. Beat in Bailey's Irish Cream.

Slowly add the flour mixture and vanilla. Mix until smooth. Pour into 2 greased 8-in. cake pans. Bake for 20 minutes. Turn out and cool on cake racks.

CUSTARD FILLING

2 eggs
¾ cup sugar
2 tbsp. flour
½ cup brewed coffee

½ cup Bailey's Irish Cream
1 cup evaporated milk
1 cup chopped pecans
2 tbsp. butter

In top of a double boiler, beat eggs. Add sugar and flour. Beat well.

Add coffee and Bailey's Irish Cream. Mix until smooth. Add milk and mix well. Place over boiling water and cook until mixture thickens, stirring constantly, about 10 minutes.

Add pecans and butter. Beat until very smooth. Let cool.

Split cake layers. Spread custard between layers.

BUTTERCREAM ICING

1 lb. confectioners' sugar
½ lb. butter

2 tbsp. Bailey's Irish Cream

In a blender, mix sugar with butter. Slowly add Bailey's Irish Cream. Mix until creamy and smooth. Spread entire cake with icing.

Serves 8.

1-2-3-4 CAKE

The only cake my mother ever knew how to make was what she called the "1-2-3-4 Cake." It was simple and gave her more time to sit at the fish pond. She loved to fish. If the fish were biting, it was a pound cake. If not . . . it was a layer cake with strawberry preserves between the layers.

3 cups self-rising flour
1 cup butter, softened
2 cups sugar

2 eggs
1½ cups milk

Sift flour twice and set aside.

Mix the butter and the sugar well. Beat the eggs and add to the butter and sugar. Mix well.

Slowly add flour, mixing in. Add milk to mixture. Beat until smooth.

Grease 2 9-in. cake pans well with more butter. Or, if you're making a pound cake, grease 1 Bundt pan. Pour mixture in pans or pan.

Bake cake pans at 350 degrees for 25 minutes, or 45 minutes for Bundt pan. Test by sticking a thin straw in center. If straw comes out clean, the cake is done. Usually, cake will leave sides of pan when done.

Serves 6-8.

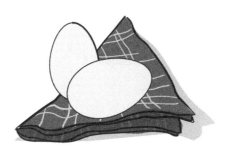

BANANA FRITTERS

4 very ripe bananas

2 cups self-rising flour

¼ cup sugar

2 eggs, beaten

½ cup milk

1 cup vegetable oil

½ cup confectioner's sugar

Peel and mash bananas. Set aside.

Sift flour into a bowl. Add the ¼ cup sugar and stir well. Add eggs and mix well.

Slowly add milk. Beat until you have a smooth batter. Stir in mashed bananas.

Heat oil over a medium fire. Drop spoonfuls of batter in hot oil. Fry fritters about 5 minutes per side until brown.

Drain on paper towel. Sprinkle with confectioners' sugar.

Serves 8.

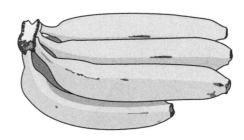

BANANA PUDDING

You can always have great memories of beautiful people by the dishes they enjoyed preparing for their families. We had a wonderful woman who worked for us at Dooky's for nearly forty years. She cooked at her house for all the Civil Rights workers, took great care of her sick mother, and was always "Madear" to her whole family. "Madear" was short for Mother Dear.

At Dooky's, she worked nights as a bartender. However, she never wanted to be called a bartender. She preferred being a barmaid. I had to do a lot of talking to convince her that, to me, a barmaid was someone who just served drinks. Instead, she was a master of her job. She was a great mixologist and could hold the attention of a bar lined with people with her great smile and honest wisdom. She passed away, and Dooky's has never found anyone to replace her.

Here is my poor attempt at her great banana pudding.

1 cup sugar	3 tbsp. butter, softened
3 tbsp. cornstarch	1 tbsp. vanilla extract
12 oz. water	36 to 40 vanilla wafers
1 12-oz. can evaporated milk	4 bananas
4 eggs, beaten	Whipped cream

Mix sugar and cornstarch. Place in a pot. Stir in water, a little at a time, until mixture has no lumps.

Place over a medium fire. Add milk, stirring well. Cook for about 5 to 6 minutes until mixture comes to a boil.

Lower fire. Add eggs, butter, and vanilla and whisk well. Stir constantly until you have a smooth custard. Take off fire and let cool.

Lay vanilla wafers in bottom of a shallow baking dish, crumbling some of them. Line sides of dish with wafers. Slice 2 bananas over wafers.

Pour half the pudding over bananas. Repeat process, ending with pudding. Place in refrigerator overnight. Serve with whipped cream.

Serves 6.

PULLING CANDY

In the winter, we always had molasses. Making this candy was our Sunday entertainment, especially when my cousin Manuela came to visit. She always made it perfectly. This takes good teeth. It is really a taffy.

2 cups molasses
1 cup sugar
1 cup water

4 tbsp. butter
½ tsp. vanilla extract
1 cup flour

Pour molasses, sugar, and water in a saucepan. Stir well. Slowly cook over a medium fire, stirring constantly until it makes a hard ball when dropped in water (about 25-30 minutes). Remove from fire.

Add butter and vanilla. Beat until mixture is smooth. Pour onto a greased baking sheet to cool.

When mixture is cool enough to handle, dust your hands well in flour and begin to pull the candy. This process works well with two people. Pull chunks of candy off the baking sheet and twist each until it becomes light in color. We would stretch candy in long, twisted ropes and then cut them into 3-in. lengths.

Serves 8.

CHOCOLATE EGGNOG

2 12-oz. cans evaporated milk
1 can water
½ cup chocolate syrup
6 eggs

1½ cups sugar
½ cup Godiva liqueur or dark
  crème de cacao
½ tsp. nutmeg

Pour milk and water in a large pot. Add chocolate syrup. Over a medium fire, slowly bring to a boil.

Separate eggs, reserving whites. Beat egg yolks well. Add sugar. Beat until well blended.

Take about 1 cup hot milk and slowly add to egg mixture. Mix well. Slowly add back to remaining hot milk, stirring constantly.

Beat egg whites until stiff. Fold into hot milk. Add liqueur, stirring gently. Serve hot or cold in mugs. Sprinkle tops with nutmeg.

Serves 6.

ORANGE WHIP

8 large eggs   **2 cups sugar**
3 oranges

Separate eggs. Squeeze oranges. Grate rinds. Set aside.

Beat egg yolks about 10 minutes. Pour into a 2-qt. pot. Add sugar, orange juice, and rind. Cook over a medium fire until mixture is creamy, about 15 minutes. Let cool a little.

Beat egg whites until stiff. Slowly add to egg mixture. Fold in well until all is mixed. Put in glass dishes. Place in refrigerator to chill.

Serves 4-6.

STRAWBERRY PRESERVES

When I was growing up, we grew strawberries, so in season we had lots of berries. Berries that were too ripe or too small to sell were called culls. We got to keep those. Mother made preserves and Daddy made the best wine in town. I never learned the wine recipe, but I always made preserves.

Mother used to say, "One pound of sugar for a pound of berries."

4 lb. very ripe strawberries   **4 lb. sugar**

Remove tops from berries and discard tops. Wash berries and drain well. Put berries and sugar in a large pot and toss gently. I like berries to stay whole if possible.

Bring to a boil over a medium fire. Let cook for about 10 to 15 minutes until sugar thickens. Be careful not to burn the sugar.

Let cool. Pour in clean jars. Store in refrigerator.

Serves 8.

TOMATO PRESERVES

3 lb. very ripe tomatoes
3 lb. sugar

3 lemons
2 tbsp. finely chopped fresh ginger

Boil a large pot of water. Dip tomatoes in boiling water. Let sit for about 5 minutes.

Remove skin and stem end from tomatoes. Cut tomatoes in wedges. Place tomatoes in a pot with sugar.

Place over a low fire until sugar melts. Slowly, bring to a boil.

Squeeze lemons. Add lemon juice to tomato mixture, stirring constantly. Add ginger. Let simmer until mixture becomes thick, about 30 minutes. Let cool. Pour in glass jars.

Serves 6.

AFTERWORD

My days come and go
Like rough seas or gentle brook.
I know joy and sorrow
And still I cook.

Whether friend or enemy
Enter this welcome nook,
Undying faith defends me
And still I cook.

Blessings abound in spaces
We often overlook.
Blessed are the satisfied faces
That urge me to cook.

My family tells me sometimes that I work too much. Maybe they just don't understand that I love the work I do. I do try to slow down every now and again, though. I like to go to the New Orleans Museum of Art just to browse through the rooms. That, to me, is time well spent. There's so much talent gathered in that one place that it becomes mind-boggling. I could look at one painting or a piece of fine porcelain for hours.

In some of the paintings, you can understand why artists say they paint because they must. It's not about the money. There's more to life than making money for money's sake. The thing you do must give you joy and peace of mind.

I'm lucky, I guess, to have made the choices I did early on. I've noticed, at times, people trying hard to be somebody else. They think they have to change who they are to be successful. I think that's a big waste of time, when they could be spending their time becoming better at who they really are.

I am a cook. Cooking is the one thing I know, and I have to make what I know work for me. It has held me in good stead for more than fifty years. I suppose it will keep me going for a few more. It's an honorable profession. The important thing for me is that it gives me pleasure.

That would be my parting advice, if anyone should want it. I'm sure others have said the same thing, and they've probably said it more elegantly. Your best bet in life is to do what brings you joy. And remember to be yourself and give your best to whatever it is you do, then use that to help others become the best they can be.

INDEX

CPSIA information can be obtained at www.ICGtesting.com
Printed in the USA
LVOW020712090213

319379LV00005B/19/P